PRAY

TO

REMEMBER

DREAMS

TELLA OLAYERI

TELLA OLAYERI

All rights reserved under International Copyright Law

Content may not be reproduced in whole or in part or in any form without consent of the publisher

Email; tellaolayeri@gmail.com
Website tellaolayeri.com.ng

US Contact
Ruth Jack
14 Milewood Road
Verbank
N.Y.12585
U.S.A. +19176428989

DEDICATION

This book is dedicated to the **HOLY GHOST** for inspiring me to write this eye opener book.

APPRECIATION

My appreciation goes to my dedicated wife, **MRS NGOZI OLAYERI,** who typed the manuscript of this book and designed the cover page. Despite the difficulties we encountered, she never lost hope.

My appreciation goes to my lovely children, **MISS IBUKUN, DAVID, MICHAEL, COMFORT and MERCY.** They encouraged me day and night as I write this book!

Respect and honor should be given to who is due. Favor comes from God and men as well. My calling (writing evangelism) met the timely support of a particular man of God, preacher, teacher, prophet and General Overseer. He awakes my inner man and gave me sound spiritual support. Without his earlier support for my first book, *Fire for Fire Prayer Book* and subsequent ones, I may not be where I am today in Christian literature writing. He gallantly stood by me in fulfillment of my calling.

This book you are holding is a testimony of my claim. This book wouldn't have seen the light of the day, if not for the spiritual encouragement I gathered from my father in the Lord who served as spiritual mirror that brightens my hope to explore my calling.

I am talking of no any other person than the **General Overseer of MOUNTAIN OF FIRE AND MIRACLES MINISTRIES WORLD WIDE, DR. D. K. OLUKOYA.**

Once again, I say thank you sir. Your support has yielded yet another earth shaking book.
THANKS
Evangelist Tella Olayeri.

HOW TO USE THE BOOK

Prayers are written at the end of each chapter of the book. Treat each topic with prayers written in the chapter. You can as well raise prayer points on your own to address your dreams.

The book is primarily divided into two parts. Read chapters one through chapter nine, mostly in the day and reserve chapter ten for night vigil. The tenth chapter has 99 decrees in all, written specifically to address issue on dream and forget. In this chapter, you may make use of anointing oil. Hence, it is advisable you have one.

Endeavor to do the night vigil, using all the Psalmist decrees. You can as well add prayers of yours according how Holy Spirit directs. Let your vigil start around 12 midnight and pray for two to three hours. If you are facing strong challenges, I advise you go for two or three days dry fasting, taking warm water, (not hot tea!), to clear your throat from drying. Do this, and be ready for quick answer to your petitions.

PREFACE

To dream is spiritual, as it foretells what is going on in the spirit. Naturally, people dream. Dream is a natural process like breathing. Dream is an extension of situation we live in when awake. Dream represents mental activity that occurs when conscious control is removed. Hidden mysteries are uncovered in the dream and if one is not in the spirit, he may not understand what the dream is all about.

The fact is you cannot prevent it from occurring as the message you need to receive is relayed to you in the spirit. Revelations passed in the sleep help the dreamer to foresee future occurrence, to serve as warning, to encourage, to reveal what is most likely to happen now, or what may happened in the past. This is the more reason we must not neglect our dream as it constitute an inter-relation between the now, the past and the future of human experience.

Anyone who can interpret dreams wisely stands better chance to plan and organize things rightly. It is an added advantage, if one dream and remember his dreams.

It is therefore a calamity not to dream, as guiding hands may be absent in your affairs. No wonder if one is deprived of his dreams; it foretells the tendency to forget good ideas awaiting him. Thus, it is logical to say, anyone who forgets his dreams, forgets assets. To have better harvest, your spiritual current need to be transmitted into physical. Many dreams are direct, and when put to practice, it brings outstanding results.

You may be among the small group who remember most of their dreams in vivid detail. This is good but it is rare anyway. You may belong to the large majority who remember only vague parts of their dreams. This is not so good. Lastly, you may belong to the sizeable group who forgets everything. This is spiritual disaster. These people forget what they dream as soon as they wake. They can best be classified as people who don't dream at all. They do not know what transpired in the spirit realm.

People that fall into this group are many. If we try to ask the question, who dream? and able to answer it correctly, we may know how large the number of people that dream. The fact is, dreamers cut across sex, age, and color. The young, the old, male and female, young and old, white, colored and black all dream. Majority of people dream to remember fragments of their dreams or do not remember their dreams at all.

It is well known that half message received in the dream cannot give valid result or information for

PRAYER TO REMEMBER DREAMS

decision making. It is good to have quality data before authentic information or message can be attained. This is the situation with dream as well. It is therefore necessary to equip yourself well to remember your dreams.

The secrets to overcome this are boldly and empathetically written in this book. Your sure success after dream is guaranteed. From here, I shall say, "You are welcome to dream world.

TELLA OLAYERI

PREVIOUS PUBLICATIONS OF THE AUTHOR

1. Fire for Fire Prayer Book Part 1

2. Fire for Fire Prayer Book Part 2

3. Bye Bye to Poverty Part 1

4. Bye Bye to Poverty Part 2

5. My Marriage Shall Not Break

6. Prayer for Pregnant Women

7. Prayer for Fruit of the Womb

8. Children Deliverance

9. Prayer for Youths and Teenagers

10. Magnetic Prayer for Singles

11. Victory over satanic house Part 1

12. Victory over satanic house Part 2

13. I Shall Excel

14. Atomic Prayer Points

15. Goliath at the gate of marriage

16. Deliverance from Spirit of Dogs

17. Naked warriors

18. Power to Overcome Sex in the Dream

19. Strange Women! Leave My Husband Alone

PRAYER TO REMEMBER DREAMS

20. Dangerous Prayer against Strange Women

21. Solution to Unemployment

22. 630 Acidic Prayer Points

23. Prayer for Job Seekers

24. Power to Retain Job and Excel in Office

25. Warfare in the Office

26. Power to Overcome Unprofitable Wealth

27. Command the Year

28. Deliverance Prayer for First Born

29. Deliverance Prayer for Good Health and Divine Healing

30. Warfare Prayer against Untimely Death.

31. Dictionary of Dreams

32. Discover Gold and Build Wealth

33. My Head is not for Sale

34. 830 Prophecies for the head

35. 30 Power Points for the Head

36. Prayer after Dreams

37. Prayer to Locate Helpers

38. Anointing for Eleventh Hour Help

39. 100% Confessions and Prophecies to Locate Helpers

40. Hidden Treasures Exposed!

41. Prayer to Cancel Bad Dreams

42. Prayer to Remember Dreams

43. 1010 Dreams and interpretations

44. 650 Dreams and Interpretation

45. 1,000 Prayer Points for Children Breakthrough

46. Emergency telephone calls of God

47. I Am Not Alone

48. My Well of Honey shall not dry

49. Shake Heaven with Praises

50 Deliverance prayer for Middle Born Part One

51. 800 Deliverance prayer for Middle Born Part Two

52. Deliverance prayer for Last Born Part One

53. 800 Deliverance prayer for Last Born Part Two

PRAYER TO REMEMBER DREAMS

Table of Contents

PRAYER TO REMEMBER DREAMS 14

DREAMERS IN THE BIBLE 25

BENEFITS OF DREAMS 41

BEWARE OF DREAM FAILURE 52

DEALING WITH DREAM ERASERS 66

DEALING WITH SPIRITUAL BLACKOUT 69

DEALING WITH FRAGMENTED DREAMS 73

THE WAY OUT 77

PRAYER OF LIBERTY 90

NINETY-NINE DECREES 146

CHAPTER ONE

PRAYER TO REMEMBER DREAMS

When God wants to reveal something about the present or the future, he frequently uses dreams and visions. God appeared in a vision to Abraham, Jacob, Samuel, many prophets, as well as New Testament Saints. Dreams with message from God could be given to his people or heathens, often in the latter cases; one of God's people interpreted the dream, Daniel vs Nebuchadnezzar. Therefore, if your spirit is not alive, you may not see visions or dream dreams.

This book is written with the belief you are new in the territory of dream Kingdom. Hence, it will be necessary to define what dream is, in a nutshell. Dream is the language through which Holy Spirit speaks to man, except for induced or manipulated ones. Dream is therefore a spiritual language of communication between man and God. Dream originates from three major sources:- God, man or, devil. What we are most interested here is dream that comes from God. The most common way God speaks to us is through dreams.

Dreams can either be direct or indirect. Direct dreams need no interpretation as it tells us exactly what will happen and steps to take. It is like being given an instruction to carry out. The case of King Abimelech is a vivid example.

An indirect dream is one spoken in parables. This type of dream is spiritually technical and may need the help of an interpreter to know what God is saying at a point in time. The dream of King Pharaoh is an example, Genesis. 4:1-7

Your dreams are raw materials in your hands to build your future. Raw materials must be converted to product or products before it can be meaningful to the owner. So it is, with a dreamer. Hence, your dreams need to be remembered and converted (interpreted) to meaningful message before you can make use of it. It is almost impossible to build, if you cannot recognize type and purpose of raw materials in your hands. A dreamer who forgets his dream is like someone with raw material but could not recognize or know he had one. The usefulness of raw material may die, if it is not utilized. Since dream gives birth to products, it then boils down to the fact that a dreamer must refine his dream.

This brings us to the mystery of spiritual refinery. Hence, you need to go into your refinery or release your spirit for one so that your dreams can stay and be incubated for remembrance and actions after sleep. Thus, dreams or trance communicates something important. It is your responsibility to decode your dream through prayers.

To dream is a spiritual right not a privilege. If you don't dream, or you dream and forget, it suggests you are losing your right to the wind. The book of Joel 2:28 says, ***"And it shall come to pass afterward that I will pour out my spirit upon all flesh, and your sons and your daughters shall prophesy, your old men shall see visions".*** Thus, your inability to dream or, dream and forget is a spiritual slap on your face. Dream is thus, divine right to mankind.

As enemies are striving hard that we might experience untimely death, unable to accomplish our race in life, so is not with God that we die in ignorance. It is a pity many die in ignorance without knowing who they are and what they should be. Life is full of struggles that sometimes yield little or no testimonies. You need to fight it out in prayer and marry your spirit to dreams that comes from above to serve, as spiritual guide in your daily activities. For this reason, you need to connect yourself spiritually to hear from God. The fact remains, you will not be excused if you mortgage your destiny on the platter of dream failure, or dream and forget syndrome. The fact is you will deny yourself of heavenly message and rights which you need to exercise when you prayer. Your dream can make you a champion, but

PRAYER TO REMEMBER DREAMS

once you do not dream, it is like living a dead life. You need freedom, spiritual revival, and resurrection from the pit of the dreamless. Today is your day, you need heavenly injection to revive your dream life, that will make you fresh, stay fresh and be an achiever.

It is high time you locate your spiritual compass and navigate into the bank of dreams for spiritual information. You need to awake and stop living in the cloud, so that enemies won't have field day in your life. Inability to dream may not empower you to detect their wickedness. Hence, you need to fetch spiritual compass and locate powers behind your dream predicaments, knowing when and how to launch counter attacks against them.

It is good you know that your inability to dream, or to dream and forget is a spiritual abnormality. It means your spirit man is weak. It means you are spiritually trapped. It means you are spiritually dead while asleep. Everyone has a spirit he uses to communicate with his creator. You have a soul that lives in your body. Your spirit is the real person in you not your physical body. It is the spirit that goes about in the dream when your body is at rest. Since spiritual controls the physical, before anything could happen in the physical it must have taken place in the spirit. Hence, if you do not dream, or you dream and forget your dreams, or, you could only retain a fraction of your dreams, it means your spirit man is not functioning well in the spirit. This may be due to the fact that your spirit man is caged or placed under spiritual arrest in the spirit. Once your spirit man is arrested or caged by dark forces, it becomes almost impossible to dream, and where you dream at all, you may forget almost what you dreamed. The fact is there are some powers assigned to remote or control your spirit man in the spirit.

For this reason, you should not brush aside failure to dream or inability to remember the dreams you dream. It is a serious matter that needs to be taken care with, with all seriousness. Hence, diagnose your dream life never take things for granted, by saying, "It is part of life".

People who suffer from forgetfulness of dreams can be divided into three categories. They are:-
    1. Those under attack of dream eraser.
    2. Those under attack of dream fragmentation.
    3. Those under attack of spiritual blackout

Really, the three above may look alike, but they are not. The first categories of people under attack of dream eraser are those who dream but could not remember their dreams after they wake from sleep. A vivid example was Nebuchadnezzar, king of Babylon, who could not remember his dream after, he wake from sleep.

The second categories are people who dream but only remember fragments of their dreams after they wake from sleep. This set of people finds it difficult to tell the start of their dream or the end of what they dreamed.

The third category, are those who experience total blackout when asleep. This people, don't dream at all. They only hear people discuss dreams but never have such experience. Such people suffer from attacks of power call dream erasers. We only mention these three categories of people that suffer this type of attack in this chapter; we shall discuss them better in later chapters.

At this point, it is good we discuss what I call dream ethics as we journey into dream the world. The first law of dream ethics is, at times dreams are symbolic which makes them appear meaningless after you wake from sleep. Here, you need to meditate on them for spiritual understanding.

Secondly, dreams are sealed instructions you need to unseal or decode before you can arrive at message or information passed to you.

Thirdly, every dream and its symbols must be interpreted in light of the life circumstances of the person to whom it is given. Thus, a dream may not be understood fully without knowing something about the life of the person concerned.

Fourthly, avoid misapplication of dreams. Sometimes friends and family members are often used as symbols. The fact is, sometimes they represent ourselves, sometimes they represent friends or family members, sometimes they represent themselves and sometimes spiritual issue like church.

Lastly, you need to know, who the dream refers to and what it is really about.
Once you know the particular subject God is talking about and who He is referring to, proper dream interpretation is usually not difficult.

Finally, I welcome you into the fold of people that dream and remember their dreams. The day of living in the cloud is over. A new dawn of spiritual enlistment has come to stay. But then, there are rules and keys you need to know before your dreams can be meaningful.
Also, there are messages, symbols, colours etc. you need to decode before relevant meanings can be given to your dreams. It is after knowing this; you will be able to correctly interpret your dreams.

To be a master in your dreams, I advise you buy my book titled **DICTIONARY OF DREAMS**. It will

PRAYER TO REMEMBER DREAMS

help you interpret your dreams and establish your feet in the spirit.

Failure to remember dreams is like living in cloud of darkness. It is a spiritual mistake to forget your dreams as it causes spiritual vacuum. You need to be a dream champion, by having ability to remember and interpret reams.

To achieve this, you must have a mind-set of a champion that will make you have an edge in spiritual pursuits. It is time you forget past mistakes hunting your destiny, for the Lord shall heal the wounds inflicted you and fill vacuum created to destroy you. One thing you should know is, even the most intelligent make mistakes, and all you need to do is to learn from your mistakes. Be honest with yourself. Listen and take to inner voice. Be real with yourself; know who you are and what you are.

The wiser you are the better you live. You need spiritual power to remember and decode your dreams. You need a mind of change today. It is a good philosophy to engineer change in your life every day. A change for advancement, and or, a change from forgetfulness to remembrance of your dreams.

Obedience, it is said, is better than sacrifice. When we obey God, we hear from Him. To show resistance or unwillingness to do the will of God makes us live in darkness. God may not speak to a person who is not willing to obey.

Until you locate direction, wandering continues. You need divine direction to attain distinction in life. You are created a star not a scar, a champion not a failure. Dream speaks volume. God's direction is loaded in dreams. When you don't dream; you lose out to failure, sorrow and rejection.

As a child of God, you posses spiritual eyes in your heart, whenever it is renewed, it speaks through your heart or show things that cannot be detected by ordinary eyes. Hence, you shall see beyond the physical, dwelling in the spirit, having dreams you cannot forget

Be happy you pick this book today for the Lord shall see you through. Your hang on to this day shall be healed. The fact remains, ability to hang on when everything is pulling apart, is the difference between a success and a failure, and between a winner and a loser. The book stands as a tool and weapon in your hands, a sure way of information to silence sleep oppressors. I pray you shall not live a life of a struggler.

As you remember your dreams and able to interpret them, pray warfare prayers to cancel

PRAYER TO REMEMBER DREAMS

every evil dream until you are done with it. The second step is, you shall decree goodness and manifestation on positive dreams you dreamed.

Lastly, bless God for giving you insight and keys to unlock your dreams and visions. By so doing, you stand better chance to get result than one who dream and remember his dream but never pray.
May God bless you. Amen.

PRAYER POINTS

1. O Lord, equip me with decoding spirit t decode my dreams.
2. Dream manipulators in the corridor of my life leave me alone and die
3. Dream Kingdom refinery in me, com alive and make me understand my dreams.
4. Spirit to remember dreams incubate my life in the name of Jesus.
5. I claim spiritual right to dream and remember in the name of Jesus.
6. I shall not die as an ignorant person that does not dream in the name of Jesus.

7. Heavenly message through dreams locate me by fire in the name of Jesus.
8. I lay my hands on spiritual compass to navigate into dream kingdom.
9. I inject my spirit man with blood of Jesus
10. Any power that cage my spirit man, release it and die.
11. Power of dream erasers, vacate my life and die in the name of Jesus.
12. Every attack I suffered as a result of dream fragmentation shall end today in the name of Jesus.
13. Light of God, arrest and disgrace power of blackout in my life.
14. O Lord, turn me to champion in dream territory in the name of Jesus.
15. Power of wilderness, troubling my life die in the name of Jesus.

CHAPTER TWO

DREAMERS IN THE BIBLE

Dream is a spiritual right and a means of communication with the heavenly. Dreams recorded in the Bible buttress the fact that God is in business of informing people through dream in the sleep. The Bible recorded a dozen dreams apart from numerous visions in the Bible. Dream serves the purpose of warning, encouragement or to give confidence in respect of issues at stake. Lessons learnt in each dream are narrated for spiritual growth. You need to read and digest each dream, to know the reason why you should pray and be free from dream blackout.

Let's go into dreams in the Bible in an orderly manner, starting from the books of Old Testament to New Testament.

DREAMER NUMBER ONE

ABIMELECH.

The first dream recorded in the Bible was that of Abimelech, the King of Gerar, Genesis 20:2. This is one of the towns Abraham stayed, when he left his father's house for the land of Canaan.

What led to this famous dream was that, Abimelech erroneously took Sarah, wife of

Abraham for wife, after Abraham told Abimelech that Sarah was his sister. Sarah being a beautiful, charming lady arrested the heart of Abimelech, and took her for wife.

Within a while, in the night, God appeared in the dream to Abimelech with a warning. The Bible recorded it. ***"But God came to Abimelech in a dream one night and said to him, "You are as good as dead because of the woman you have taken. She is a married woman" Genesis 20:3.***

King Abimelach never wasted time, but returned Sarah back to Abraham, in the presence of his officials. He never stopped there, but gave Abraham a thousand shekels of silver as a recompense for his wrong act!

At this time, God closed the womb of Abimelech's wife and his slave girls. With God's direction, Abraham prayed for Abimelech's household and they were healed.

The Bible passage revealed a number of things to us. Firstly, it was a warning dream that rebuked Abimelech and his likes from committing adultery.

Secondly, his dream made us to understand, that Abraham was a prophet, Genesis 20:7; and a prayer warrior of great repute, Genesis 20:17.

Thirdly, it teaches us that God's eyes monitor, guide and save people from danger.

DREAMER NUMBER TWO.

JACOB

Jacob had two dreams recorded in his favor in the Bible. The first dream occurred when he went towards Haran as charged by his father to take a wife among Laban's daughters. He got to a place and make stone for his pillow when night came. As he lay down to sleep, he had his first dream. The Bible records it. *"And he dreamed, and behold a ladder set up on the earth and the top of it reached to heaven: and behold the angels of God ascending and descending on it" Genesis 28:12.*

In the dream, God appeared to Jacob with the promise that He God shall pass inheritance of Canaan to Jacob and his seed. God finally fulfilled this promise when the Israelites occupied Canaan.

The second dream of Jacob can best be described as a dream of freedom. After serving Laban for several years, he was given Leah and Rachel as wives. It got to a stage, when plans of Laban to cheat Jacob backfired. He taught he could placed Jacob into permanent slavery by promising him, cattle's that are of ring streaked, speckled, and grisled, Genesis 31:10.

This verse summarized actions taken in heaven, in support of Jacob against slavish intensions of Laban against Jacob. Heaven supported Jacob, as Jacob took bold steps, and initiatives to let it come to pass. The verse above confirms the statement, "whatever will happen in the physical will first happen in the spirit". This was what happened in the case with Jacob, as he took bold steps in the physical to actualize what God did in the spirit.

Jacob's dreams taught us many lessons. The first dream was a message of hope, support and future fulfillment. In the dream, Jacob knew God was with him. His objectives, purpose, focus and goals for the future started with this dream. He knew God's plan for him and his offspring. If he was the type that doesn't dream or have no dream memory, he may not know God's plan for him.

The second dream testifies to God's support for Jacob. While angels of God did the spiritual aspect, Jacob carried out practical aspect of it. If Jacob had been a man with dream failure, his service to Laban would have been a wasted one. He would have served him for years unending. This was what Laban had in mind before he went into agreement with Jacob. At last heaven rose in Jacob's support in the dream. Jacob dreamed and was able to interpret it and took right step. The step he took brought liberty to him life and his household.

DREAMER NUMBER THREE.

LABAN

Laban was Jacob's father-in-law. Jacob served Laban for several years before he decided to leave for Canaan. On hearing that Jacob fled with his two wives and household, Laban was furious, and pursued after Jacob for seven days. He and his brethren overtook Jacob in mount Gilead. In the night, God appeared to Laban warning him not to do anything wrong with Jacob. The Bible records it. ***"And God came to Laban the Syrian in a dream by night, and said unto him, take heed that thou speak not to Jacob either good or bad" Genesis 31:24.***

This dream saved Jacob from Laban and his brethren's hands, that joined in pursuit against Jacob. If dream wasn't in existence, Jacob may have lost his life that day. The dream Laban had, sticked to his memory bank as he applied the warning he received in the dream. If Laban had been someone that dream and forget his dream, he may kill Jacob in annoyance. The race called Israel today may not have been in existence today! Thus, dream failure is an architect of problems.

DREAMER NUMBER FOUR.

JOSEPH

Joseph was one of the twelve sons of Jacob, born to him by Rachel. Joseph's dreams were proverbial and symbolic in nature. He had two dreams which have almost the same meaning.

The first dream concerned his supremacy above his brothers, while the second one combined, his parents and brothers doing obeisance to him in the dream. Both dreams brought wrath against him from his brothers. The Bible records them.

DREAM NUMBER ONE.
"For behold, we were binding sheaves in the field, and, lo, my sheaf arose, and also stood upright, and, behold, your sheaves stood round about, and made obeisance to my sheaf" Genesis 37:7.

DREAM NUMBER TWO.
"And he (Joseph) dreamed yet another dream, and told it his brethren, and said, Behold, I have dreamed a dream more; and behold, the sun and the moon and the eleven stars made obeisance to me" Genesis 37:9.

The two dreams of Joseph nearly sent him to untimely grave, but God saved him from the hands of his treacherous brothers. His dreams gave him focus even in the midst of temptation. His dreams eventually came to pass when he became Prime Minister in Egypt. It was then; he could interpret his dreams to the letter.

DREAMER NUMBER FIVE.

THE BUTLER AND THE BAKER.

The butler and the baker were of Egyptian origin who served as chief cup bearer and baker of the King, Pharaoh respectively. Their dreams were related to Joseph who interpreted the dreams correctly.

The Bible recorded manners and time of the dreams. *"And they dream a dream both of them, each man his dream in one night, each man according to the interpretation of his dream, the butler and the baker of the King of Egypt, which were bound in the prison" Genesis 40:5.*

Their dreams came to pass as interpreted by Joseph. They knew their fate and the judgment ahead of them as interpreted by Joseph. Thus, it is good you know how to interpret dreams, so as to know step to take in your undertakings. It is good you buy my book titled **DICTIONARY OF DREAMS,** to give you insight to dream interpretations.

DREAMER NUMBER SIX.

PHARAOH

Pharaoh was the King of Egypt. He had two different dreams in one night. In the first dream he saw seven fat cows coming out of the Nile grazing among the reeds a while after, another seven emaciated cows came out of the same Nile and devoured the seven fat cows. Then he woke.

That same night, he fell asleep again and dreamt of seven heads of grain, healthy and good, growing on a single stalk. After them, seven other heads of grain sprouted, thin and scorched by the east wind. The thin heads of grain swallowed up the seven healthy, full heads, then Pharaoh woke.

The two dreams disturbed his heart not until he got an interpreter to his dream, in the person of Joseph, the Hebrew, imprisoned for no just cause. The importance of Pharaoh's dreams are many. Firstly, it saved Egypt from starvation after it was rightly interpreted by Joseph.

Secondly, it saved Jacob (father of Joseph) and his entire family from starvation as they eventually migrated to Egypt, where they found solace.

Thirdly, it brought about the fulfillment of Joseph occupying high position of Prime Minister, making his father and brothers do obeisance to him! What he dreamt at seventeen came to pass at last.

Lastly, the dream metamorphosis into fulfillment of God's prophecy that the descendants of Abraham shall be enslaved in foreign land, which later came to pass.

In conclusion, this asserts that dream is powerful, truthful and a role model in the spirit, if it can be rightly interpreted and remembered. If Pharaoh was unable to remember his dreams, many souls may have lost during the seven years famine revealed to him in the dream. Joseph may have died in prison as well, if he did not have ability to interpret the dreams. Thus, it is good to remember and interpret dreams.

DREAMER NUMBER SEVEN.

THE MIDIANITE.

Gideon the warrior was to lead Israel against the Midianites, the Amalekites and other eastern peoples who settled in the valley, described with the phrase as thick as locust in Judges 7:12. In order to purge Gideon's fear, God directed him to go into the camp of the enemy at night! Gideon obeyed.

As he carried out his surveillance, a midianite soldier narrated his dream to his friend, which was interpreted as Midianites falling prey to Gideon. This dream encouraged Gideon to strike, which he did. God gave the enemies into his hands. Thus, the dream brought fear into the heart of the enemy but strengthen the Israelites.

DREAMER NUMBER EIGHT.

KING SOLOMON.

After King Solomon offered sacrifice to God in Mount Gibeon, God appeared to him in the dream, to ask for whatever he wanted. Solomon did not missed words, he asked for a discerning heart to lead the chosen children of God, Israel rightly. His demand in the dream pleased God. He gave Solomon discerning spirit he asked for and added to it. He said, since Solomon never asked selfishly by asking for personal riches, long life or the death of his enemies, He, the Almighty God, shall give him riches, honor, and long life as well if Solomon followed his command as did David his father. Thereafter, Solomon wake from sleep.

It was a direct dream that doesn't have difficulty to interpret. It was more or less, a conversation in the sleep with God that later came to pass. Righteousness is one of the basic ingredients to see face of God. When Solomon woke, he knew God was in his support. This gave Solomon encouragement and focus during his reign. Solomon excelled as promised by God. No one on earth was recorded as wise as him; neither can his riches be compared with anyone. Thus, he was famous and rich.

DREAMER NUMBER NINE.

NEBUCHADNEZZAR, DANIEL 2:4

Nebuchadnezzar was the King of Babylon, who dreamed terrible dream, and thereafter could not sleep. He summoned all the wise men in Babylon, the magician, enchanter and astrologers to tell and interpret his dream. They couldn't, except an exile from Judah named Daniel, who did.

Daniel enquired of the Lord, to reveal unto him the dreams of Nebuchadnezzar. The dream was that of a large statue, enormous, dazzling and awesome in nature which was interpreted to mean political situation that shall take place in future.

This dream opened door of honour to Daniel, and other three Hebrews, Shadrach, Meshach and Abednego. While the three were made administrators over the province of Babylon, Daniel remained at the royal court to administer along with the king there. Daniel's ability to unravel the mysteries, brought him to a further limelight in a foreign land.

DREAMER NUMBER TEN.

JOSEPH- HUSBAND OF VIRGIN MARY

Joseph, husband of Mary the virgin had three different dreams recorded to him. His first dream concerned his surprise of the conception of Mary his newly married wife, who he never slept with. He was contemplating how to quietly divorce his newly married wife, when he had a dream, warning him to accept the pregnancy as it was of the Holy Spirit. In the dream, the sex of the baby was given (male), the name (Jesus) and his mission on earth (to save his people from their sins). This dream sealed the marriage, which Joseph intended to quietly dissolve. A baby boy was put to bed by Virgin Mary and was named Jesus, the Savior, Mathew 1:18-25.

His second dream was recorded in Mathew 2:13, concerning appearance of an angel of the Lord who forewarned Joseph of impending danger of plans to kill Jesus. The angel told Joseph to depart immediately and escape to Egypt, and stayed there until he was told the next step to take. Joseph was in Egypt until after the death of King Herod who sought to kill Jesus.

The third dream was, when an angel of the Lord appeared to Joseph in Egypt to leave for Israel, which he did.

The three dreams concerned the conception and safety of Jesus. If Joseph was a man who dream not, or the type who dream and forget his dreams, no one knew what may have become of the savior. Thus, to be troubled by spirit of dream and forget is bad.

DREAMER NUMBER ELEVEN.

THE THREE WISE MEN

The three wise men came from the East to give presents to the newly born baby, Jesus. To further their enquiries of where to find the boy, they went to King (Herod) who was bitter in mind to hear of the arrival of a new king in his kingdom. He sent the magi away, to make a search for the baby so that he might go and worship him. Really his plan was not to worship, but get rid of the baby.

The magi were warned in a dream not to go back to Herod. They later returned to their country by another route, Mathew 2:12. Although, the magi erroneously revealed the King of kings to Herod,

God saved the baby through dream. If the Magi suffered from dream and forget syndrome, what would have been the fate of Jesus? Dream and forget is therefore dangerous.

DREAMER NUMBER TWELVE.

PILATE'S WIFE

The close of dream in the Bible was that of Pilate's wife, who sent message on behalf of Jesus to his husband, Pilate the judge. According to custom, it was the governor's custom at the feast to release a prisoner chosen by the crowd. A decision was to be made of who should be released to the crowd between a notorious prisoner, called Barabbas and Jesus.

Pilate the Judge was sitting on the seat when a message came from his wife saying, ***"Do not have anything to do with that innocent man, (Jesus), for I have suffered a great deal today in a dream because of Him" Mathew 27:19.*** Her dream was a confirmation of Jesus innocence, even in the thick of hatred against him.

In the dreams treated so far, one salient point is, dream is a channel of information to human beings. It can be during the day or at night. But most dreams occurred at night in the Bible. This does not mean that facts or information's cannot be passed during the day when men slept.

PRAYER POINTS

1. Power to communicate with heavenly fall upon me in the name of Jesus.
2. Dreams that gives direction of purpose appear in my sleep in the name of Jesus.
3. O Lord, empower me to take bold and right steps in the physical as support of what I dreamed
4. Thou plan of God for me appear in my dream for quick execution.
5. O Lord, give me keys to interpret dreams in the name of Jesus.
6. Every temptation that will enslave me to dream blackout expire in my life in the name of Jesus.
7. O Lord, give me power that will make enemy surrender in the name of Jesus.
8. I shall not wake into hands of death in the name of Jesus.

9. My talent of promotion appear in the name of Jesus.
10. O Lord, let me trample upon my enemies on the head in the name of Jesus.
11. I shall excel in all my undertakings in the name of Jesus.
12. O Lord, give me talent to unravel mysteries in the name of Jesus.
13. Dark river shall not swallow me in the name of Jesus.
14. Thou spirit of dream and forget in my life die in the name of Jesus.
15. O Lord, fill my heart with wisdom in the name of Jesus.
16. I shall not reap dangers of dream and forget in the name of Jesus.

CHAPTER THREE

BENEFITS OF DREAMS

Dream and forget, and or, inability to dream is a spiritual calamity, likened to a person who can't remember his name or home address. Dream blackout is often the origin of this spiritual emptiness that leads to frustration, stagnation disappointment, and utter despair. Dream world is a different spiritual place in its entirety. There, all kinds of transactions take place between the sleeper and the spirit world.

Dream is a spiritual source to tap spiritual message, power, blessings, favor and mercy necessary to promote our well being. Godly spirit, and or, angels deliver messages in the dream. People who dream and remember their dreams are blessed with opportunity to know what is going on in the spirit. Such is not the situation with people who doesn't dream at all, or with people that dream but forget their dreams as soon as they wake from sleep. The fact is, when their prayers are answered, they may not know, as dream blackout may take over their hearts with fear and depression of negative thoughts.

Secrets hidden away from men may not be known if one doesn't dream. Great ideas flow in the spirit through dreams. Many great things start in the dream. Many knotty problems are solved in spiritual blackboards as well. As a result, from sleep God unravel solutions. No wonder it is said, is anything too difficult for God? The answer is, No. Your sleep is therefore profitable if you dream, recollect and interpret them.

Another vital reason why it is good to dream and remember is, it often reveal spiritual balance sheet and status of the dreamer. When you ask God what you weigh in the spirit, He will show you. God will make known to you, where you faired and where you failed in the race of life. He is the Master where you are the servant. He is the Father where you are the child. Thus, you are answerable to Him. A son or daughter can go to his/her father to know how he or she faired. It is the same, when you go to God to know your spiritual status. If you don't dream, or you forget what you dreamt, it may be impossible to know your spiritual status, and or, steps to take to improve your lot in life.

The question that readily comes to mind is, if you do not dream, how can you know what God wants you to accomplish in life? It is your responsibility to pray and ask God to reveal relevant facts and figures that will benefit you. When you tell God to reveal what you are, and what to pursue in life, you will pray while God answers through dream. A lot of things may go wrong with your spiritual life, which may hinder you from progressing. This can

PRAYER TO REMEMBER DREAMS

be known if you dream and remember your dreams. The question now is, if you do not dream at all, or you dream and forget, how can you know? The fact remains, the spirit controls the physical. Thus, if you have talent to dream, elevation will find you out, as revelation of who you are in the spirit can place you in good position.

It is fatal not to dream at all, or forget dreams you dreamed. The way God communicates with people mostly in the Bible was through dreams. God revealed to Joseph of the Old Testament what shall become of him in future. What he dreamt eventually came to pass as he occupied the seat of Prime Minister in Egypt in later years. Through dreams, Joseph of New Testament saved his marriage, the life and our believe in Jesus Christ as our Lord and Savior. If the two Josephs have problems of dream and forget, or they don't dream at all, Joseph of Old Testament may lose direction, whereby Israel as a race may not exist. Pharaoh got wind of impending starvation against Egypt through dreams, even though he could not interpret his dreams. If Joseph of New Testament failed to dream, or is the type that forgets dreams, no one would have believed Jesus was conceived of the Holy Spirit. The Bible reveals that in the past, God spoke through dreams to saints and sinners alike, warning them, directing them, and or, helping them. If the two Josephs were the dream and forget types, and or, they don't dream at all, what may have been their faith? Inability to dream, or recollect dreams are a sure way of heading to an unknown destination. My question now is, are you heading from grass to grace in the spirit, or from grass to grave?

The primary purpose of dream is to give divine revelation to the dreamer. The Holy Spirit reveals secrets to people so as to frustrate plans of the enemy. Dreams can take you back to your childhood and reveal havoc done to your foundation. In such dream, Holy Spirit gives keys of direction and what needs be done to advance your life.

Dreams and visions speak and re-direct steps needed to take by the dreamer. It can tell you to leave your present job or habitation for alternatives. It can tell you to make certain adjustments in your dealings for better result, all in the name of dreams and visions.

Enemies often gain easy access to attack non-dreamers, and or, people that fail to remember their dreams. It is easy for night raiders to raid sleeps and privacy of such people. Since they don't know of sleep molestation or harassment, their bodies become easy access for dream rascals. Since there is no resistance, they freely attack such body. Thus, when you do not dream, or you dream and forget your dreams, it gives spiritual robbers opportunities to empty you spiritually. They can therefore, steal your marriage, steal your virtues, glory, job and whatever their hands find in you.

Candidates that fall under dream and forget banner are often exposed to disjointed, fragmented and un-coordinated life. They hardly live a focused life, since they do not know when they were attacked. Also, they hardly know when God provide answer to their demands. They believe everything come by chance.

Your inability to dream, or to dream and remember may not allow you be a partaker in activities in the spirit. Hence, you may not have ability to monitor, pray, or change certain events that may devalue your life.

The knowledge of your environment and habitation can be known through dream as well. Many are living a borrowed life today as a result of satanic house they occupied. If they are able to dream and remember their dreams, they won't be under such captivity.

To live in a wrong house, connotes living a wrong life. Whatever good, you lay your hands upon may not be profitable simply because, you don't dream to know the bad or warning signals ahead of you. Your dream life which would have been spiritually guided is exposed to danger of wicked arrows. The danger of this is that you will be tossed about by wind. You won't apply comma where you should, neither apply full stop at appropriate time.

The advantage of dream and recollect is to enable you be loaded spiritually and take right step at the right time in the right direction. When you dream and forget, such opportunity may elude you.

In dream, there is what we call spiritual negotiation. It is the ability and process to go into prayer to reverse, delay, fast forward or cancel prophetic revelations in the dream. Hezekiah prayed against death prophesied against him, instead of death God added more years to his life. A dreamer may foresee fulfillment of his ambition to be far off or inconvenient, as a result call upon God to fast forward it into fulfillment. This is done through prayers, when such dream is replayed for adjustment. It can be done by praying prayer of reversal, or prayer of moderation that moderates dreams for better. Although, God knows better, the Bible says, ask and it shall be given. You can know the end of a situation in the dream, and with prayer, alter it to suit your expectations. It is good you perfect every transaction in the dream to advance your life. You can do this, if you can remember your dreams.

Some dreams are classified as warning dreams. They are loaded with warnings for the dreamer to

PRAYER TO REMEMBER DREAMS

take caution concerning present matters or with future. Such dreams may not be good enough to the dreamer; hence he needs to know steps to take to advance his life. In a situation where you do not dream or you forget your dreams, it may be impossible to know warning signals ahead of you.

When you suffer from dream memory loss, your advancement and breakthrough may hit the rock along the line. You may experience obstacles of walls of stagnation, sea of trouble, and various forms of delays. Such hindrances may be revealed to you in the dream the fact that you don't dream makes you dwell in dream wilderness.

Souls are summoned, prosecuted and jailed in the spirit. Really, person so affected may be going about his business but may not get result as expected. Such person meets failure here and there, and is loaded with complaints and sorrow. He is married to stagnancy and delay in whatever he lays his hands. If you are the type that dream and recollect your dreams, you can rise up to the task in prayer to cancel and nullify wicked judgment passed against you. By this, you can pray targeted prayers, rather than pray empty or general prayer. Thus, inability to dream and remember your dreams, or, dream and remember fragmented parts of your dream is dangerous.

The fact remains that souls are either recruited for evil, invaded, manipulated or satanically controlled by defiant spirits. The aftermath effect is that people so affected may experience difficulties, obstacles, hindrances and reverses if radical spiritual steps are not taken. If you are the type that does not dream or you dream and forget, it may be impossible to know when you are manipulated in the spirit or when your territory is invaded by wicked agents of darkness.

Ability to remember dreams give Christians opportunities to take right steps in the right direction with the choice to either accept or reject the dream. Bad dreams are bad, while good dreams are good. Bad dreams are rejected, cancelled, nullified or sent back to sender. This can be achieved by praying violent prayers, and or, apply blood of Jesus. At times, you may call upon fire of God to arrest the situation to consume wicked instruments fashioned against you. On the other hand, when you dream good dreams you can claim them for fulfillment and manifestation.

Hence, you need to take action by telling God to lead you right. To dream good dreams, and fold your alms without taking step to actualize it is bad. You must work and walk into your treasure of habitation. God wants you to act with faith by taking prophetic steps. When Abraham dreamt, he took step of faith and became father of nations.

PRAYER TO REMEMBER DREAMS

When Solomon dreamt, he took step of faith and became the wisest man in the surface of the earth, so you must take step of faith, anytime you dream good dreams.

Above all, it is a calamity to dream and forget as you may be cheated in the spirit unnoticed, or stay long in the wilderness of life. But, if your eyes, mind and heart are alive in the spirit, revelations from above shall propel you into dignity.

PRAYER POINTS

1. Grip of spiritual blackout in my life die in the name of Jesus.
2. I shall not remain stagnant in spiritual matters in the name of Jesus.
3. Lord, empower me to have upper hand in spiritual matters in the name of Jesus.
4. Lord, reveal my spiritual balance sheet to me in the name of Jesus.
5. Power to dream and remember my dreams fall upon me in the name of Jesus.

6. Lord give me keys of direction in my dream in the name of Jesus.
7. Every spiritual robber assigned against my destiny die in the name of Jesus.
8. I shall not dwell in the wilderness of dream in the name of Jesus.
9. Every dark sentence against my soul be nullified in the name of Jesus.
10. My dreams shall enable me walk into the treasure of my habitation in the name of Jesus.
11. My destiny be affected for good in the dream in the name of Jesus.
12. Power of spiritual communication fall upon me in the name of Jesus
13. I arise from sleep failure to sleep abundance in the name of Jesus
14. O Lord, you are the unchangeable changer change my dream life by fire
15. Blood of Jesus, cleanse marks of impossibility in my life in the name of Jesus

PRAYER TO REMEMBER DREAMS

16. My lost glory in the sleep, come back in the name of Jesus

CHAPTER FOUR

BEWARE OF DREAM FAILURE

Anyone who doesn't dream can best be described as a walking corpse. It is like living an unfulfilled life, as it may be difficult for him to communicate with his creator in the spirit through dream. It is therefore dangerous to dream and forget, and or, not dream at all. For example, if you were dragged into a slaughter house for witchcraft judgment in the dream, you may not know. If you were slaughtered in the dream, which leads to untimely death in the physical, it may be impossible to cancel such dream from fulfillment.

If you are sentenced in the dark court of the enemy, you won't know. If blessing is coming your way, and Prince of Persia countered or confiscate it in the spirit, you won't know as well. You experience such predicaments simply because you do not dream.

There are reasons that lead to inability to dream, or remember dreams which shall be discussed fully in this chapter. When you keep forgetting your dreams, you need to address powers stealing dreams from your memory. There are two major causes of memory loss; they are often grouped as personal or demonic.

PRAYER TO REMEMBER DREAMS

Personal memory loss is caused mainly as a result of drunkenness, glutton attitude, sin, wrong counsel and stress. Others shall be mentioned and grouped under demonical influence of dream memory loss. Let's treat the causes below one after the other.

DRUNKENESS: This is the attitude of taking alcohol in excess. Drunkards lose senses and ability to control their behavior. He loses respect among men and in the spirit. Whatever he does is counted senseless by people. His sleep is not worthy as he becomes inconvenient on bed as a result of toxic running through his blood stream. Such situation makes him experience desert sleeps, compounded with memory loss.

Anyone found in this condition, may find it difficult to remember his dreams. It is like opening doors of his life wide to demons to operate unmolested. His body becomes unresisting to attacks. He foams in the mouth and smelly to angels expected to pass heavenly message to him. Thus, his attitudes close every door of blessing and opportunities which might be revealed to him in the dream. His heaven becomes brass, surrounded with walls of darkness. Thus, a drunkard can best be described as a living dead person.

GLUTTONY: A glutton is a person who eats too much. To be possessed by glutton spirit is bad.

Victim becomes weak and sleepy anytime he over eats, in the day or at night. Whenever a person is overtaken by glutton spirit, he becomes mad for food. A glutton has an insatiable appetite for food. He eats whatever comes his way. He eats anywhere, anytime and anyhow. He is easily possessed and fed in the dream, simply because he never knew how to say, No, when it comes to food!

Anyone possessed by glutton spirit hardly fast, to seek the face of the Lord. Whenever they mistakenly fast, they break with variety of foods consuming both heavy and light foods at a time. In sleep his body is weak, ir-resistant to attacks. Such person hardly have meaningful dream and where message is passed in the dream, he forgets everything as soon as he wakes.

The fact is, his spirit could not match with spirit of God for spiritual understanding.

EVIL COUNSELLORS: Another cause of dream and forget is when one is fed with words of discouragement from evil counselors. There is nothing bad in having spiritual father in the Lord, spiritual mother in the Lord, spiritual sister or brother in the Lord, and or, spiritual friend in the Lord.

What matter most is, how spiritual the person is. Is he or she spiritually balance in the spirit? Can he or she be a good counselor in time of need? Unfortunately, many of these so call spiritual father, mother, brother or sisters are confuse on how to treat matters relating to dream and forget issues. You may hear them say, "God created you that way" "I know of someone facing same fate as yours, many years back" "Yours is not new, many are like that". Thus, several discouraging comments are said to discourage you from thinking about it. They are not wicked anyway, it is only that your so called father in the Lord, mother in the Lord, or sister and brother in the Lord, are equally ignorant of what to do or say.

DOUBT AND UNBELIEF. This is one of the major tools readily available to strengthen forgetfulness of dreams. There are people who do not belief in dream and so do not dream at all. There are people who doubt its existence, thereby put off their minds from it. Hence, they don't dream at all, or best, they dream and forget. Rather, they argue that dream is a bunch of meaningless riddles and enigmas, which shouldn't be taken serious. Such people are caged by unbelief and miss what might have been communicated to them in the spirit.

SIN: - Righteousness makes a man, sin kills soul of men. You may be in dream and forget saga if you bury yourself in sins. God communicates with only those who are on the same spiritual wave length with Him. This happens when you walk in the spirit; put aside all filthiness and wages war against flesh. Lust associated with casual sex and promiscuity pave way for easy attack. Angels of God may find you unfit for visit, hence he may hold on to your dream message. Thus, if you are not visited, you may not dream.

One can be weighed down in the spirit as a result of carriage of loads and weights. Sin is a load. The moment you keep on sinning you are adding evil load on your head. The more you sin, better you are in the hand of Satan. In as much you are in his care, he can do whatever he wants with you. In such position, Satan can turn your back against the Holy Spirit. He can place dark cotton wool on your face and ears, thereby making you inaccessible to God in the dream. By this, you may not hear from God or see vision any more, which makes you an empty vessel in the spirit. You are therefore empty before God, but loaded with sin that makes you a cheap instrument in the hand of Satan. Hence, you break and destroy Communication Bridge between you and God. You are now on your own!

Spiritual weakness is a weapon that causes forgetfulness in dreams. At this point, it is as if your spiritual candle is burning out, instead of being aggressive in the spirit, you lose interest.

Your spiritual interest starts fading, unlike the start of the morning when you were serious and aggressive in church activities. Suddenly, your seriousness with God's work suddenly drop, prayer meeting becomes uninteresting while bible reading or study becomes a problem. At this point, your spiritual thermostat breaks down, cutting you from the spirit world of God. Hence, dream becomes scarce in your sleep and, where you dream, you quickly forget, making you a dead person in the spirit, lacking understanding of what to do after sleep. The book of Proverbs 21:6a rightly describe the situation when it says, ***"The man that wandered out of the way of understanding shall remain in the congregation of the dead"***

STRESS: - Stress is a condition that causes hardship or disquiet of mind as a result of pressures. Anyone suffering from stress is often exposed to danger of fear and troubled mind. He becomes uncoordinated in matters arising. A stressed person becomes weak even in sleep. As a result, whenever he dreams, it is either revealed after sleep either disjointed or forgotten.

Stress is a gradual killer. It kills flesh and mind without previous warning. It cages one from taking extra mile to achieve beautiful results. When mind is stressed, brain and memory bank is not left out.

In the sleep, memory bank becomes weak and sometimes empty. As a result, in dream kingdom, such person becomes helpless and useless before enemies battle ready to raise attack against his memory house. Once subdued, whatever dream that comes his way in sleep is either forgotten or remembered in disjointed or fragmented manner, and or, in meaningless form. Thus, stress add no value to dream life, rather it saps and purge memory banks of a dreamer.

WHEN PRESSED DOWN IN THE DREAM: - To be pressed down in the dream is a gate way to spiritual humiliation by the enemy. The aim of the enemy is to ensure you are in a confused state of mind all the time. Hence, he adopts satanically oriented means to purge, and sap you spiritually. They oppress in the spirit and ensure it manifest in the physical. They press you down in the sleep and bring your spiritual zeal and effectiveness to zero level. As one is pressed down, his spiritual being becomes weak thereby affect his dream memory. When he wakes, he may remember being pressed down but may not remember anything that follows thereafter.

What may have served as dream bank is affected as whatever he dreams is forgotten. He becomes a shadow of himself. Even if he remembered, it is only fragment part of it, he could remember. The simple reason he could not recollect is that fear, dread and confusion has taken over better part of his body and reasoning faculty.

When you are pressed down in the dream fear of the night fills your heart. The Bible says your sleep shall be sweet but the enemies will say, No. Such powers arrest souls and harass them in the dream. Such powers can be called environmental forces or household wickedness. They attack memory banks of people and make things difficult for them. They make victims walk around breakthroughs without fulfillment.

CURSE: - A curse is a word, phrase or sentence calling for punishment, injury or destruction of something or somebody. It is a violent language against a person. Curse is never uttered for good intention. It is an act taken either out of vengeance, jealous or wickedness to unleash terror on a person. Thus, one can unknowingly be under a curse issued. Curse makes one suffer and experience misfortune and ruin in the course of time.

Curse is a satanic statement spoken against a person to cause him reverses life. Good memory is a blessing from God, but enemies fight hard to alter it. Such alteration causes delay in his thinking faculty. Wicked souls can place hidden curse on people either in the day or at night .Charms and incantations are used to perpetrate this against unsuspecting victims. Sometimes your biological data (name of the mother, and or, father) are part of instruments used to facilitate such evil acts. They strike by cursing you and your sleep.

If a person is not prayerful enough, he may discover that his dream life suddenly seized, where he is opportune to dream; only a fragment of it is remembered. At the end, he will not be able to fashion out his dream in concrete term or by description. He will be confused and unable to narrate his dreams in detail. Curse will not only paralyze your dream life but shall make you unfit for spiritual battles.

INCISION: - This is an act that has multiple effects on a person. Incision is the act of cutting your body, rubbing it with satanic powder, blood or leaf materials for a purpose. It is believed, it has seal against advances of powers or attacks of the enemy. Incision can be equated to covenant. Most incisions in the body or on the head attract blood. When blade or sharp object is used to mark the body or any part of the head, blood will come out of such part so cut. What is rubbed on such surface is either blood of a fowl, pigeon or animal. There is a sort of blood covenant un-noticed by the person involved.

When your head is marked as narrated above, and rubbed with satanic powder or blood, a message is passed to the brain. Since you do not know the content of substance rubbed on your head, it will be difficult to reject its effects. Satan doesn't give free gift. Hence, you are bound with silent agreement you know nothing about. He may as a result corrupt your dream memory, cause you memory blackout, or apply spiritual eraser against your dream system whereby, you won't remember your dreams at all, which serves as price paid for the protection you received through incision. He has every legal ground to claim this against you because you are now at his mercy.

Incision can thus be linked with dream memory loss. As it is often said, it is better not to know Satan than share tent with him. Many who are captivated by dream memory loss are architects of their predicaments.

LAYING OF EVIL HANDS: - The laying of evil hands on your head in the spirit or in the physical, may rob you of your visions and dreams. A victim may lose his dream memory this way, if cornered by such demonic personality. When you are noted to be gifted, attacks may come in different forms, including strategy to wipe out your dream magnet. They are satisfied once your memory bank is rendered bared.

There was this man I met some years back who suffered loss of vision as a result of evil hands laid on him. He said, he was under priesthood training when the incidence happened. At tender age, he use to see visions and was gifted in dreams. His vision was accurate as A, B, C, while his dreams came to pass as if it was pre-arranged. He said one day, his master called him to his office, gave him bitter kola to chew and lay hands on his head and made some silent statements which he could not hear. After this, he told him to go. This man said, ever since this encounter, he dreamt no more, while vision becomes scarce commodity in him By the time he narrated little story of his life, one can easily see poverty and wretchedness boldly written on his face.

Many lost their talents, visions and dreams this way. It takes grace of God for such people to regain their spiritual being if affected this way. For such people, the Joseph in them may suddenly die, while Daniel in them may disappear unannounced. Hence, they become empty men and women in the kingdom of dreams and visions as their talents are punctured or polluted by wicked ones. In the case of the gentleman narrated above, he lost his divine baptism of dreams and visions unannounced!

EVIL BARBERS: - Dreams can be affected as a result of criminal acts of evil barbers assigned against ones sleep. In the spirit hair represents glory. Therefore, whoever tampers with your hair tampers with your glory. Hence, your thinking faculty may be affected as it has direct relationship with the brain. It therefore means, barbing, weaving, adulteration of anything that affects hair in the spirit may affect your dream life. Anytime attack is unleashed, it may start as temporary problem, but later become permanent problem of not dreaming at all.

When strange fellows barbed you in the dream, it portends wicked acts of stealing goodness from your destiny, your memory bank included. Once a thief steals from someone, it becomes almost impossible to collect it back from him. At this point, war of recovery comes in. While victim felt bitter and go into prayer to recover what he lost, enemy is bent from releasing it. The focal aim of enemy is to use instrument of bewitchment to erode victim's memory, and introduce sorrow, demotion and emptiness into his life. Such are the tragedies of evil barbers in the dream.

EVIL SCALES AND VEILS ON THE FACE: - A covered face knew no direction. A blind man, it is said, cannot lead a blind fellow or else both will fall into the pit.

When a face is covered or tied with dark cloth or band, darkness is introduced into such life. Signal of blackout is sent to the "memory house" of the victim. The effect is, his vision becomes blurred, while heavenly message to him becomes corrupted. Once this is achieved, a vibrant dreamer is captivated, never to remember his dreams any more.

PRAYER POINTS

1. Power of dream failure leave me alone and die in the name of Jesus.
2. Every sentence passed against me in dark court be nullified.
3. My dreams sealed in the spirit, receive freedom in the name of Jesus.
4. Any power stealing dreams from my memory be arrested by the power of the Holy Ghost in the name of Jesus.
5. Every pollution in my blood blocking me from receiving heavenly message die in the name of Jesus.
6. Anything in my life that put off angels of God from visiting me, leave alone and die in the name of Jesus.

PRAYER TO REMEMBER DREAMS

7. Every attitude in me, that will make walk about like a living dead person die in the name of Jesus.
8. Glutton spirit in me die in the name of Jesus.
9. Evil counselors quit my life and let breathe of dreams locate me
10. Every doubt and unbelief that is making me swim in dark oceans die in the name of Jesus.
11. O Lord, empower me to wage war against flesh in the name of Jesus.
12. Owner of evil load carry your load and die in the name of Jesus.
13. Arrow of stress against my soul backfire in the name Jesus.
14. Every talisman power that rob me of dreams expire in the name of Jesus.
15. Every curse pronounced against my sleep life backfire in the name of Jesus

CHAPTER FIVE

DEALING WITH DREAM ERASERS

Dream erasers are agents of darkness that attack people with spiritual blackout. They attack and erase dreams from memory of victims. The normal thing after sleep is to dream and remember your dreams, but this is not so with many. They are denied such opportunity as a result of attacks against their memory banks. Anyone so attacked is left empty and spiritually powerless, in matters relating to dreams and visions.

To receive message and retain it while asleep becomes almost impossible. Enemies of sleep cause memory loss on victims and ensure they don't remember what they dreamed. They sow seeds of forgetfulness in the lives of victims and paralyze their spiritual awareness. Someone who use to dream with accuracy may suddenly turn a dullard in the territory of dream kingdom. As a result, warnings he ought to receive in the dream seized, as nothing is remembered again.

Such attacks equally affect people who use to dream before, but suddenly becomes candidates that lost their dream track records. They exposed to empty sleeps, counting sleep liabilities, instead of sleep assets, that add value to life. Their sleep balance sheets are often in red, where liabilities swallow assets in sleep.

In time past, such people are good dreamers, but suddenly they lost out. The fact remains, their spiritual eye glasses got broken or stolen by wicked ones in the spirit, leaving them in the cold hands of dream failure. Hence, they lost their spiritual right to dream, remember, or receive message from above.

They eventually become story tellers, telling stories of how they use to dream with accuracy in the past.

Dream erasers contribute grave spiritual multiplier effects on people. They reduce victims to valley of life and encroach on their spiritual liberty. They often have landslide victory on people unchecked. The fact is, hope is not lost, as there is power in prayer. Today, you shall apply your spiritual right to pray and get result, as it is your right to dream and remember your dreams.

Hence, we shall go into violent prayers below and destroy wicked agents assigned against your dream life. After praying the prayer points, you shall go and pray all prayers written in later chapter of this book, titled **PRAYER OF LIBERTY**.

PRAYER POINTS

1. I inject blood of Jesus into my memory bank in the name of Jesus
2. Spiritual blackout, leave my life by fire in the name of Jesus.
3. I shall not be an onlooker where dreams are discussed in the name of Jesus.
4. O Lord, let my story change today in the name of Jesus.
5. Dream generator in my body, awake, come alive in the name of Jesus.
6. My spirit being receive energy from heaven in the name of Jesus.
7. Anywhere my spirit is caged; receive energy from heaven in the name of Jesus.
8. I shall not dine with agents of blackout anymore in the name of Jesus.

CHAPTER SIX

DEALING WITH SPIRITUAL BLACKOUT

Dream spiritual blackout mean emptiness caused by dream erasers in the memory of people. Spiritual blackout foretells inability to dream when asleep. People so affected find it difficult to give accurate definition of dream, as they don't dream at all, and or, forget what they dreamed. Such people often hear others discuss dreams, but don't experience such in sleep. They lack what generate dreams in the sleep. Their memory bank is empty.

As in economics, the law of demand and supply applies to memory banks in the spirit. Memory banks demand spiritual information from above in the spirit and is given out (supply) to the dreamer after sleep. It is when these apply, that is, spiritual principle of demand and supply, a dreamer is opportune to remember his dreams and find meanings to them.

To realize this noble objective is what Satan hates. His agenda is simple, to keep you in dream wilderness. Really he may keep your spiritual generator (soul) alive, but shall cage it from operating rightly when victims are asleep. Thus, enemies can allow your spiritual electric current (soul) work, but not connecting. People so caged, cannot receive signals from the spirit realm as their souls are caged in the prison of darkness. Hence, such person becomes spiritually weak.

Anyone who suffer from spiritual blackout can be likened to an electric generator suppose to be in good working condition which lack supply of light. Really the generator may be working fine, but due to one technical fault or the other, light may not be generated. Also, every electrical and mechanical aspects of the generator may work fine, but bulb that supplies light may not be there. As a result, for one reason or the other, blackout exists. Such is the situation with memory blackout.

In every blackout nothing good comes to play. Anyone so affected, may not carry out spiritual assignments as expected. Blackout cause spiritual restrictions as victim may not know steps to take on issues on ground, even when he prayed, as his medium of communication is either polluted or erased. His management style will be affected, making his moral value and thoughts low. Dream blackout is bad. It encourages evil and multiplies energies of evil doers. It is in such situation, night raiders operate, troubling souls unchecked.

It is common for dark agents to place evil seal on people's memory to hinder them from carrying out spiritual communication with the heavenly. When such seal is placed, victims experience dream

PRAYER TO REMEMBER DREAMS

blackout. Hence, such victims is denied spiritual package God has for them.

When the spirit of a dreamer is caged or imprisoned, it becomes almost impossible for him to dream and remember. Once his spirit is caged, he will experience spiritual blackout as his spiritual memory bank is affected. Dark agents or powers can cause blackout in one's life when the spirit is caged or imprisoned in dark rocks, evil forest, dark water, inside an animal, and or, in any part of dark kingdom operating against your life. When a victim is so caged, he may find it impossible to dream.

As a result of evils perpetrated by dark powers and the effects felt, strong step and prayers need to be said. To address this issue, you shall pray a number of prayer points below. Thereafter, you shall go to later chapter of this book titled, **PRAYER FOR LIBERTY**, which address every issue concerning, dream and forget. By the power of the living God, after praying these prayers you shall remember your dreams clearly, as you remember your names!

PRAYER POINTS
1. Spirit of dream paralysis leave me alone and die in the name of Jesus.

2. Spiritual vacuum in my life be sealed by the blood of Jesus.
3. My brain receive spiritual revival in the name of Jesus
4. Every fear that cause darkness in my life expire in the name of Jesus.
5. My spirit be connected to heaven in the name of Jesus.
6. O Lord, heal my wounds in the name of Jesus.
7. Blood of Jesus, kill every poison in my heart in the name of Jesus
8. Holy Spirit divine intervene in y situation in the name of Jesus.

CHAPTER SEVEN.

DEALING WITH FRAGMENTED DREAMS

People affected by fragmented dreams often suffer from dream fragmentation and lost in recounting dreams. They forget most of their dreams as soon as they wake from sleep. They knew quite well they dreamed while asleep, but they could not recollect them after sleep. They often complain, "I remember only few of my dreams". While many in this category recollect half of what they dreamed, some hardly remember a quarter of theirs. Really, they dream, but can't remember all. This is a fatal spiritual error that gives Satan opportunity to dangle his wicked hammer against destiny of people through dreams.

Mostly when dreams are in fragments, it becomes almost impossible to deduce picture out of it. Brain becomes dry, while mind is troubled. Anxiety rules the mind, fear rules the heart. The spirit, soul and body become un-coordinated. To recall events and words spoken in the dream becomes almost impossible. Only fraction of what they dreamed is remembered, thereby causing them wounded spirit among dreamers.

A wounded spirit never co-ordinate well. When mind is hurt, you hardly recollect what you dream after sleep. Constant hurts, heartbreaks, and sorrow can poison the spirit, which may eventually lead to bitterness, hatred, un-forgiveness and malice.

This may rule your heart and cause blockage against spiritual messages in sleep. This is so, because it is almost impossible for such spirit to co-ordinate with Holy Spirit in the dream. Hence, your spirit man may not hold together messages and information passed in the dream. As a result, you will often see yourself remembering your dreams in fragments, disjointed and un-coordinated.

There are powers attached to such attacks in the spirit. People in this category may have suffered from serpentine bites or spits that affects their eyes in the spirit. Also, they may have encountered evil breeze that paralyze memories of people. Some may experience blow of evil dust into their eyes, thereby making it impossible for them to figure out what they dreamed. Anyone so affected this way may experience broken link with God through dreams.

If you know you suffer from fragmented dreams, I strongly advise you take to the followings. First, do not rush out of bed when you wake. Try as much as possible to stay calm and quiet on the very part of the bed you slept. Do not rush out of bed as other events may interfere with your meditation!

PRAYER TO REMEMBER DREAMS

The second step is, as you are on bed, have your eyes closed with a set mind, praying in tongues, concentrating on the Holy Spirit for spiritual intervention.
Before you know it, lost dreams will come like a flash! It is the work of the Holy Spirit.

PRAYER POINTS

1. Every attack against my dream life scatter in the name of Jesus.
2. Every arrow of darkness fired against my sleep backfire in the name of Jesus.
3. Dream robbers leave me alone and die in the name of Jesus.
4. O Lord, equip me for signs and wonders in my sleep in the name of Jesus.
5. I possess my right to dream in the name of Jesus.
6. Every wicked hammer fashioned against me break in the name of Jesus
7. Every plan of the enemy to arrest my brain in the spirit scatter in the name of Jesus.

8. My buried talent be exhumed in the name of Jesus.

9. Every arrow of diversion fired against my destiny backfire in the name of Jesus.

10. Every arrow of pollution fired against my destiny backfire in the name of Jesus

11. Every gang up to abort my plans in life scatter in the name of Jesus.

12. Oh my soul corporate with God against Satan in the name of Jesus.

13. Spirit of holiness incubate my life in the name of Jesus.

14. I refuse to be cheap article in the hands of the enemy in the name of Jesus.

CHAPTER EIGHT

THE WAY OUT

Inability to dream and remember is not a spiritual matter one should fold alms and look elsewhere. It is high time this issue is addressed with sincerity, seriousness and action. Really, answer must be provided to this ugly spiritual issue call dream memory loss. I say, again, there must be a way out of this spiritual mess.

The fact remains; there are lots of organized crimes going on in the spirit world. What takes priority in the scale of preference of Satan and his agents in the dark world is how to fashion instruments of war and wickedness against the sleep of men. They know once a victim is attacked and captured in his sleep, his fall becomes an easy walk over. These days, enemies are wild against innocent souls. Arrows of memory loss are fired on daily basis against unsuspecting victims. Complaints of memory loss in sleep are common and agonizing as stories are told and heard. Cries and complaints of, "I cannot remember my dreams anymore", and, "I can only remember few, and not all the dreams I dreamt", are common today.

Hearts are disturbed. Souls are languishing in captivity. Many were robbed of dreams and visions. Their goals and visions cannot be accomplished any more. In the light of this, everyone concerned must rise to the task and fight every power causing dream melancholy in the spirit. Strategies and wiles of the wicked against our sleeps must be nipped in the bud. We must curtail every activity of dream criminals pursuing souls about in order to harm them. Hence, radical spiritual step must be taken to address this issue. Something must be done fast now, delay may be dangerous. I say again, it is now, not tomorrow.

Therefore, put on full armor of God for warfare prayer. Stand firm and never fear. Dress up as a combatant soldier of God. Put on the belt of truth, buckled around your waist, with breastplate of righteousness in place, your feet dressed with heavenly boots to match upon every cobra and scorpions to death. Put on heavenly helmet on your head, hold sword of God in your hands ready for battle. Let your heart be clear, and fear no more. Above all, take up the shield of faith, so that you might dream and remember your dreams. Pray the prayers in this book and be ready for an answer. Wicked powers behind your dream trauma shall vacate your life and die.

The battle line is drawn. You must rise, move and go to the gates of the enemy and posses your possession, possess your right to dream, and recover what you lost in the past as a result of memory lost. Hence, you must rescue yourself from every form of wicked hammer fashioned against your sleep.

The plans of the enemy against your success are many. Their plan is to arrest your brain, bury your talents, swallow your glory, frustrate your plans, divert your destiny, assault your personality, demote your destiny, reverse your objectives, pollute your life, empty your treasure, molest and harass you in the spirit, delay your progress, abort your plans, press you down at will, plant sickness in your body, prosecute and jail you in the spirit, and what more, highjack your star and kill you.

It is time you draw battle line against dream raiders assigned to raid your sleep at will. They are wicked, merciless and faceless. They do evil with pride and arrogance. They project themselves into dreams of people, and wreck untold havoc against their destiny. Questions that may likely strike your mind are what can be done to destroy wicked tact of the enemy? Can there be hope at the end of the tunnel? Is it possible to recover from the hook of dream and forget syndrome? The answer is, yes, there are ways out. What we shall study in this chapter will give us relief from panic of dream and forget syndrome.

The first vital instrument is to **pray and be released from spiritual vacuum of dream and forget syndrome**. As a Christian, you need to spend time with God, since prayerlessness makes the old man (flesh) rise above spirit man that makes one helpless in the hands of dream criminals.

It is difficult to know mind of God without spiritual revelation. You need to **straighten your future, making your soul ready for dreams**. To straighten your future starts on your knees through prayer. Pray and be in the spirit all the time. Not until you are in the spirit, you cannot connect the voice of the spirit. You need to be spiritually loaded. Spiritual code is the language of the spirit. Just as man hears man, monkey hears monkey, snake hears snake, and birds hear birds, so do spirits hear spirit. Once regenerated spiritually, you are linked with God in the spirit, making your dream clearer and retentive.

One thing is to dream, another thing is to remember what you dream. After this comes ability to decode dreams. Hence, **you need ability to decode what God is saying**, as most messages are revealed to us in coded languages. It is when you are able to decode your dreams, you will know meanings attached to it and the prophetic steps you need to actualize or fulfill them. Dreams form spiritual warehouse of information in the spirit. When we wake, we tap from this information warehouse and find meanings to our dreams. Thus, you can't develop information from empty treasure; you must dream and remember your dreams, culled from information dream box in you. The quality of your dream memory, coupled with ability to interpret them, determines the quality of output generated from your dreams.

Brethren, you need to **pray prayer of transformation and be transformed** from dream mediocrity to a dream master. You must be a champion in dream interpretation in the manner of Joseph who interpreted dreams with accuracy. To achieve this fit, you should be born again, far from sinful acts. It is said, **"God formed us, sin deformed us, Christ transformed us".** As you are transformed, forget about sins of yesterday, think how you can build yourself into the laps of Christ today, as tomorrow shall solve itself. Know this, yesterday is dead, tomorrow never come, today is therefore the most important day in your life. It is good to be born again now (today), for Christ's transformation.

Another way out is to **pray Holy Spirit intervention prayer**, asking Him to bring back dreams or visions you forget. It is high time you call on Him to refresh your memory against dream attacks. When your memory is refreshed, your dream life shall improve considerably. Do not fold your alms looking other way, rather take prompt action. Pray against blind powers of demonic spirits. Pray against spiritual cataracts and glaucoma. Wage war and attain spiritual independence. The earlier you pray against dream erasers assigned to frustrate the fulfillment of your destiny, the better.

To obtain direction through dream, you shall open your eyes, ears and hearts to God. Put **aside all filthiness of the spirit and of the flesh** that may stand as hindrance against you. Avoid every form of contamination. Learn to tune into heavenly wave length, if you must catch His voice. Our God is holy, He speaks to holy people.

There is need for you to **overhaul your environment with prayers and anointing.** Take vigilance of where you sleep. Take audit of your sleep life as well. Ask questions like, do I dream and forget in this house or where I slept last. Do I dream and recollect my dream, before now? Do I experience any strange attack? The fact remains; there are some locations that negatively influence dreams of a dreamer. Such place must be sanctified and cleansed to avoid further attacks and occurrence of deficiency. Pray the prayers that will overhaul you as well. Therefore, sanitize your bed window, doors, walls and roof as well against night raiders. Once your habitation is cleansed, your dream life would change for good. You will start to remember your dreams as if your past experience was a lie.

PRAYER TO REMEMBER DREAMS

Another major instrument for a way out of dream and forget syndrome is to **write down your dreams when you wake**. This should be done immediately you step out of bed. The fact is, many remember their dreams when they wake, but the moment they open their mouths and greet or discuss, they forget almost what they dreamt. They will struggle to remember, but it won't come!

In such situation, I advise you write your dreams as soon as you wake from sleep. To achieve this, every night before you sleep have a pen and paper, booklet or journal titled, "Personal Dreams" or "My Dreams", beside you on your bed, or under your pillow. By doing this, your writing materials will be reachable as quickly as possible. When you write your dream this way, it makes you remember it in greater detail. When you record your dreams, include each dream with date and location, whether at home or on vacation. By recording a dream and what it appears to mean you can check back later to see if you are correct in understanding its meaning or not. This also appears to be the safest and quickest way to learn how to interpret dreams correctly.

Another vital way out of this spiritual vacuum of dream and forget syndrome is to **have personal audit concerning your dream life**. By so doing, audit the last dream that led to your predicament.

What you see, observe or collect in the dream may affect your dream life.

CASE STUDY NUMBER ONE

A sister said she use to dream and remember her dreams with accuracy word for word and action for action. Her dream were like visions, whatever she dreamed came to pass like snapped pictures. It always happens as dreamt, even where it concerns other parties. According to this sister, her story changed when she dreamt of receiving presents of empty jars in the dream. Her mistake was when she woke from sleep, she never cancelled the dream or pray to nullify it. The fact is, she could not even decode the dream not after many years have passed. The sister never knew that empty jar represents emptiness and frustration. The empty jars she received in the dream was proverbial, meaning, her memory house is henceforth emptied of dreams. Ever since she collect the empty jars in the dream, her problem of dream and forget started. It was when she went for counsel and violent prayers she was able to regain her lost memory in dreams.

CASE STUDY NUMBER TWO

A brother who does not suffer from dream and forget problem, suddenly found himself caged when he had this terrible dream. He dreamt where he was attacked by evil breeze in the dream. According to him, he experienced paralyses in the left region of his hand, living his eyes blind, while his left hand and legs paralyzed in the dream. When he wakes from sleep, he could faintly remember what happened in the sleep. He never took it serious, but cancelled it with light chocolate prayer and went about his normal business. The target of the enemy was to paralyze and destroy his dream memory, which they did. Ever since the day he dreamt this horrible dream, he never dream a single dream again! His memory bank has been affected.

Dream paralysis is a satanic projection that cripples social, spiritual, emotional, financial and marital destinies. Hence, anyone who dreamed of paralysis need to seek for resurrection power of Jesus to visit any area of his or her body so affected. This is another method Satan use to sponsor emptiness into people's life.

Also, you need to **be a disciplined soldier of Christ.** Discipline is the soul of an army. You are either a man in need or a needed man to put things straight for others. When you know your personal responsibility, it will challenge you to grow. If you must conquer the world, you must first conquer yourself. You must not live your life anyhow or anywhere. You must not go anywhere without sound mission. You must not sleep anywhere you find yourself. Do not live a life without boundary. Avoid every broad and wide ways that lead to destruction. You become cheap by going for cheap things. Nothing is cheap or free. The air you breathe is free, but you dare not live or move close to polluted environment having free but polluted and dangerous air to breath. The Bible says, narrow is the way to life, broad is the way that leads to destruction. This is saying you must have boundary in whatever you do. A life without boundary ends in failure. It is the boundary that guides our ways. It is better you break the yoke, before it breaks you. If you are not disciplined, you end up as a man of no value. Brethren, I say again be disciplined.

Another vital instrument you can use to retain your dream is to **read the Word.** When you receive revelation (Rhema) in God's word, the word carries power to guide and attract Holy Spirit unto your life. When you are renewed by the Holy Spirit, your spirit man awakens to life, making your dream real and firm. It is good you allow your mind to think about things of God. Expose your life to the Word, and the Holy Spirit shall dwell in you.

Also, **build a mind that welcomes message of God through dreams**. Tell God to redesign your mind and heart for visions and dreams. The mind is where design is made. Here you need to build your heart for design. If you don't dream, you may not have accurate design to propel you into greatness. This is the reason why you must remember your dreams all the time. You must be a metamorphosis in life. As you renew your mind, you shall experience spiritual growth. The raw material in your hands and your design ability in spiritual refinery gives fine designs that will elevate you as architect of good things that befalls a man.

Apply operation a do it yourself approach. No one can make a failure of you, but you. Your best is still in the future, not yesterday. Whatever the situation, forge ahead and move forward by fire. The fact is, no one can feed on your behalf; you need to feed yourself. No one can go to toilet for you; you need to do it yourself. No one can drink on your behalf; you need to drink water yourself. No one can dress on your behalf, you need to dress up and go about your daily activities. You cannot delegate your responsibility to others, or else, you lose out. It is you that need to cry out to God for spiritual visitation and power; spiritual awakening and success.

Another vital way out of dream and forget is to **reject and kill powers behind your predicaments.** If you notice you suddenly lose track of your dreams after sleep due to attack, call upon fire of God to consume every power behind such attack. Reject and return every strange thing given you or used which caused it. Use authority which God invested in you to cancel, reject, command or issue a decree against it.

At last, you shall be a winner!

PRAYER POINTS

1. O Lord, equip me with heavenly armour, in the name of Jesus.
2. I shall be a winner in any battle I encounter in the name of Jesus.
3. Any power holding on to my instrument of greatness release me and die in the name of Jesus
4. Every wickedness in high places against my dream, die in the name of Jesus
5. O Lord, let power of resurrection incubate my dream life in the name of Jesus.
6. O Lord, clear tears of dream and forget in my face.
7. Every gang up against my dream life scatter in the name of Jesus

PRAYER TO REMEMBER DREAMS

8. Sword of God cut to pieces powers assigned against my sleep in the name of Jesus
9. Sleep wars vacate my life in the name of Jesus.
10. O Lord, convert dream blackout in my life to visions.
11. Any power assigned to corrupt my dream life die in the name of Jesus.
12. 12 Anything in me, giving enemies rooms to operate in my life die in the name of Jesus.
13. Night terrors in my life die in the name of Jesus.

CHAPTER NINE

PRAYER OF LIBERTY

This prayer session is meant for you. You are advice to pray all the prayer points in the 24 tittles first during the day, before praying anointed prayers and decrees of Psalms that follow at night. These prayers should be prayed with concentration and seriousness.

PRAYER TO REMEMBER DREAMS

LIBERTY PRAYER NUMBER ONE

THANKSGIVING UNTO THE LORD

Give thanks to the Lord, for he is good
His love endures forever.
Give thanks to the God of gods
His love endures forever
Give thanks to the Lord of lords
His love endures forever
Psalm 136:1-3

PRAYER POINTS

1. I thank you Lord for sparing my life in the midst of battles in the name of Jesus
2. I thank you in advance O Lord, for the battles I shall win, in the name of Jesus.
3. I thank you O Lord, for the mercy and protection you have upon me, in the name of Jesus.
4. I thank you Lord, for you shall not allow my prayers be in vain, in the name of Jesus.
5. I thank you Lord, for your light shall shine upon me, in the name of Jesus.
6. I thank you Lord as you shall bring revival in my dream life in the name of Jesus.
7. I thank you Lord, as you shall turn every effort of the enemy useless, in the name of Jesus.

8. I thank you Lord, for you shall make things work for good in my life, in the name of Jesus
9. O Lord, I thank you because you are mighty and bigger than my dream troubles.
10. I thank you Lord, because you are perfectly reliable.
11. I thank you Lord, as King of kings and Lord of lords.
12. I thank you Lord, for the fresh anointing you shall pour upon my life and destiny in the name of Jesus.
13. I thank you Lord for your marvelous support concerning my dream life, in the name of Jesus.
14. O Lord, I thank you because you shall not allow my memory bank go empty, in the name of Jesus.
15. I thank you Lord for the salvation of my soul, in the name of Jesus
16. I thank you Lord for intervening in my situation by fire.
17. O Lord, I thank you for being my redeemer in the name of Jesus
18. I thank you Lord for protecting me from the snares of the enemy.
19. I thank you Lord because you are my comforter in time of distress, in the name of Jesus.
20. I thank you Lord for lifting burden off my shoulder, in the name of Jesus.

PRAYER TO REMEMBER DREAMS

NOW SING

**THANK YOU JESUS
YOU ARE THE OWNER OF MY SOUL
ALPHA OMEGA YOU ARE WORTHY TO
BE PRAISE
IN ALL GENERATIONS THERE IS NO ONE
LIKE YOU
ALPHA OMEGA YOU ARE WORTHY TO
BE PRAISE.**

LIBERTY PRAYER NUMBER TWO

FORGIVENESS OF SIN.

"He who conceals his sins does not prosper but whoever confesses and renounces them finds mercy".
Proverbs 28:13.

PRAYER POINTS

1. O Lord, I call for the forgiveness of my sin, forgive me O Lord, in the name of Jesus.
2. O Lord cleanse the temple of my heart so that your spirit may dwell in me in the name of Jesus
3. O Lord, forgive me of every sin of unrighteousness in me in the name of Jesus
4. Lord Jesus baptize me with spirit that will not engage me in rebellion in the name of Jesus.
5. Lord Jesus, show justice of mercy upon me in the name of Jesus
6. Forgive me Lord, let my prayer ascend to heaven in the name of Jesus.
7. Forgive me Lord of my present and previous involvement in idolatry in the name of Jesus.
8. O Lord, control my thoughts from receiving evil command in the name of Jesus

PRAYER TO REMEMBER DREAMS

9. O Lord, forgive me of every ancestral sin that may stand against me in prayer in the name of Jesus
10. O Lord, save me from sins that chained me to one spot in the name of Jesus.
11. O Lord, let my spirit man hate every form of sin in the name of Jesus.
12. Lord Jesus, quench my thirst for sin in the name of Jesus.
13. Lord Jesus, use your blood to cleanse every mark of impurity on me that may invite sin into my life in the name of Jesus.
14. O Lord, let anti-repentance spirit dwelling in me die in the name of Jesus.
15. Lord Jesus, wash me clean of all filthiness that may stand against me on the day of judgment in the name of Jesus.
16. Lord Jesus, wash me clean of all filthiness that may stand against me on the day of Judgment in the name of Jesus.
17. Lord Jesus by your power pull me out of environmental pollution in the name of Jesus
18. Lord Jesus, remove every form of power of iniquity from my life in the name of Jesus.
19. As east is far from west so shall sin be far from me in the name of Jesus
20. As north is far from south so shall sin be far from me in the name of Jesus

LIBERTY PRAYER NUMBER THREE

EMPOWER YOURSELF WITH HOLY GHOST FIRE

Sing this song with all seriousness.
HOLY GHOST FIRE FALL ON ME
FIRE, FIRE FALL ON ME O, O, FIRE
HOLY GHOST FIRE FALL ON ME
FIRE, FIRE FALL ON ME O, O, FIRE

PRAYER POINTS

1. Holy Ghost Power, fall on me and expel from my body every stranger in my life, in the name of Jesus.
2. Holy Ghost Fire, come down heavily into my habitation and kill dream devourers harassing my destiny in the name of Jesus.
3. Holy Spirit divine put a new song in my mouth, in the name of Jesus
4. Holy Ghost, come to my aid and refine my dream life in the name of Jesus.
5. Holy Ghost Fire, go to the root of my destiny and uproot what was never planted by God dwelling in it in the name of Jesus.
6. Holy Ghost, vomit fire and cause deliverance in my life, in the name of Jesus.
7. Double thunder, double fire, locate and kill wicked sowers assign to sow evil seed in my life, in the name of Jesus.

PRAYER TO REMEMBER DREAMS

8. I purify my sleep and dreams with divine fire, in the name of Jesus.
9. Heavenly earthquake, shake and destroy habitations of the enemy in the corridor of my life in the name of Jesus
10. I arise and secure freedom by fire from the claws of night raiders tormenting my dream life in the name of Jesus
11. Holy Ghost Fire, surround me 24 hours every day against torments of the enemy in the name of Jesus.
12. Holy Ghost Power, encourage and empower angels assigned to guide me while I sleep, in the name of Jesus.
13. Holy Ghost, make me a conqueror in my sleep, in the name of Jesus.
14. I command every liquid in my body to carry Holy Ghost Fire in the name of Jesus
15. Holy Spirit Divine, take control of my sleep life, in the name of Jesus.
16. Holy Ghost Fire, take action and let every stranger fade away and be afraid out of their close places in the name of Jesus
17. Holy Ghost Fire, keep the lamps of my life burning, in the name of Jesus.
18. Holy Ghost Power, lay hands of fire upon me and purify me by fire in the name of Jesus.
19. Holy Ghost Fire, chase darkness far away from my life in the name of Jesus.

20. Holy Ghost Power, hand over banner of liberty unto me today in the name of Jesus.

PRAYER TO REMEMBER DREAMS

LIBERTY PRAYER NUMBER FOUR

COVER YOURSELF WITH BLOOD OF JESUS.

"——and when I see the blood, I will pass over you"
Exodus 12:13.

PRAYER POINTS

1. I cover myself with blood of Jesus, for protection and advancement in the name of Jesus
2. Blood of Jesus make mark in my door post and drive every enemy on evil mission to harm me in the name of Jesus.
3. Lord Jesus, circle my beddings with your blood in the name of Jesus.
4. I soak myself in the pool blood of Jesus.
5. Blood of Jesus, flow in my vain and kill every evil deposit troubling my destiny's in the name of Jesus.
6. I sprinkle and soak the garden of my life with precious blood of Jesus.
7. I immunize my life and destiny with blood of Jesus
8. I fumigate and saturate my environment with blood of Jesus.
9. Blood of Jesus, suffocate to death every stranger assigned to kill my dream memory in the name of Jesus.

10. Thou unpolluted blood of Jesus; heal me to my foundation in the name of Jesus.
11. Blood of Jesus, kill every form of satanic deposit in my body in the name of Jesus.
12. Every Satanic messenger, I blindfold you with blood of Jesus in the name of Jesus.
13. Blood of Jesus, kill every effect of hardship and failure introduced into my life in the sleep in the name of Jesus
14. Blood of Jesus, place permanent stop on tribulations in the sleep in the name of Jesus.
15. Blood of Jesus, purge every pollution and bewitchment against my life in the name of Jesus.
16. I plead the blood of Jesus, upon my life and beddings in the name of Jesus.
17. I soak my name, my destiny, and my beddings in the pool blood of Jesus.
18. Blood of Jesus, protect me from evil attack in my sleep and in the dream.
19. Blood of Jesus, silence every rage of witchcraft against my sleep and destiny in the name of Jesus.
20. O Lord, let your blood be a source of healing power to my spirit, soul and body in the name of Jesus.

PRAYER TO REMEMBER DREAMS

LIBERTY PRAYER NUMBER FIVE

ANOINT MY HEAD OH LORD

It is written, *"The spirit of the Lord is upon me, because he hath anointed me to preach the gospel to the poor, he hath sent me to heal the broken hearted, to preach deliverance to the captives, and recovering of sight to the blind, to set at liberty them that are bruised."*
Luke 4:18.

PRAYER POINTS

1. O Lord, anoint my head afresh for signs and wonders in the name of Jesus.
2. Holy Ghost Power let your fresh fire anointing take over my life for dream explosion in the name of Jesus.
3. O Lord, let my life draw strength from your throne in the name of Jesus.
4. I drink oil of the lamb, and restore my dream memory by fire in the name of Jesus.
5. My father, my father, make me a vessel of your message, in the name of Jesus.
6. Miracle power of God, overshadow my head, for dream and re-collect in the name of Jesus.
7. O Lord arise, cleanse me in and out in the name of Jesus.

8. Lord Jesus, transform me for signs and wonders in the name of Jesus.
9. Oh Lord, let your healing power chase darkness out of my life in the name of Jesus.
10. Holy Spirit Divine, visit and fill me heavily for dream success in the name of Jesus.
11. Anoint me O Lord, to deliver captives from the dungeon in the name of Jesus.
12. Anoint me O Lord and let me recover my spiritual eyes in the name of Jesus.
13. I claim victory and freedom in my sleep in the name of Jesus.
14. Anointing of God, kill every evil deposit on my head in the name of Jesus.
15. Dream killers! I am now a new creature, touch me and die in the name of Jesus.
16. By the anointing, all former evil patterns shall die in the name of Jesus
17. By the anointing, the pattern of the heavenly is upon me in the name of Jesus.
18. By the anointing, every pattern of blackout in me shall expire, in the name of Jesus.
19. By the anointing, I am a champion over my entire Goliath in the name of Jesus.
20. By the anointing, I shall excel and remember all my dreams in the name of Jesus.

PRAYER TO REMEMBER DREAMS

LIBERTY PRAYER NUMBER SIX.

BIND THE BINDERS AND LOOSE THE LOOSABLES.

It is written, ***"I will give you the keys of the kingdom of heaven, whatever you bind on earth will be bound in heaven, and whatever you loose on earth will be loosed in heaven" Mathew 16:19***

PRAYER POINTS.

1. I bind every power that bind my dreams in the name of Jesus
2. Any power holding on to my dream, I bind you in the name of Jesus.
3. Satanic band assigned to cause blackout in my memory catch fire and roast to ashes in the name of Jesus.
4. Any power assigned to turn my life upside down, you are a liar, therefore die, in the name of Jesus.
5. I cancel and nullify bad dreams working against my destiny in the name of Jesus.
6. Every dark spy assigned against me, break in the name of Jesus
7. Chain of darkness assigned against me, break in the name of Jesus
8. Chain of stagnancy assigned against me, break in the name of Jesus

9. I loose myself from every inherited bondage in the name of Jesus
10. I bind all anti-deliverance powers fashioned against my dream life in the name of Jesus.
11. Agents of confusion loose your hold over my life in the name of Jesus.
12. Agents of blackout in my life, loose your hold over my life in the name of Jesus
13. I bind anti-testimony forces fashioned against me in the name of Jesus
14. I bind every spirit working against answers to my prayers in the name of Jesus
15. Armies, of heaven bind every power delegated against me in the name of Jesus
16. I loose my blessings in captivity and receive them by fire in the name of Jesus
17. All powers that are bent on doing me harm, receive paralysis and die in the name of Jesus
18. Every reinforcement of darkness against me scatter, in the name of Jesus
19. I loose my dream life hanging in air in the name of Jesus.
20. I loose myself from the bondage of dream captivity in the name of Jesus.

LIBERTY PRAYER NUMBER SEVEN

PRAYER TO REMEMBER DREAMS

DREAM RAIDERS MUST DIE

"Arise O Lord! Deliver me, O my God! Strike all my enemies on the jaw, break the teeth of the wicked."
Psalm 3:7

PRAYER POINTS

1. Heavenly bulldozer arise and clear every power assigned against my dream life in the name of Jesus.
2. Every unfriendly friends assigned from the pit of hell to paralyse my dream life, be exposed and be defeated in the name of Jesus.
3. Every household enemy assigned to destroy my communication link with God die in the name of Jesus.
4. O Lord arise in your anger and break the teeth of the wicked in the name of Jesus.
5. O Lord, arise and strike all my enemies on the jaw in the name of Jesus
6. I order confusion into the camp of dream raiders warming up to attack me in the sleep in the name of Jesus.
7. I barricade myself against attacks of dream raiders in the name of Jesus.
8. Lord Jesus, render useless bullets and ammunitions used to torment me in sleep in the name of Jesus.

9. Stubborn pursuers against my life summersault and die in the name of Jesus
10. Dream raiders, keep distance from me or else you shall roast to ashes and die in the name of Jesus.
11. Dream raiders, I transfer failure in my dream to you in the name of Jesus.
12. Every loot, dream raiders forcefully collect from me in the dream I recover back in the name of Jesus
13. I prophetically possess my spiritual right tampered with by dream raiders in the name of Jesus.
14. I command all demonic spirits transferred into my life through demonic raiders to be withdrawn and cast into fire, in the name of Jesus.
15. I convert every dream disappointment to harvests of dreams in the name of Jesus
16. All demonic organized networks against my spirit being scatter in the name of Jesus.
17. Spirit of madness, fall upon night raiders troubling my soul, render them useless in the name of Jesus.
18. O Lord, let the counsel of wicked men assigned against me backfire in the name of Jesus.
19. I speak woe to rebellious spirit of the enemy in the name of Jesus
20. I sweep away the wicked in the corridor of my life in the name of Jesus.

PRAYER TO REMEMBER DREAMS

LIBERTY PRAYER NUMBER EIGHT

WOE AGAINST EVIL SOWERS.

"But while slept, his enemy came and sowed tares among the wheat, and went his way"
Mathew 13:25

PRAYER POINTS

1. Any power sowing evil seeds to kill my dream memory die with your evil seed in the name of Jesus
2. Profitable seeds in my life shall not be swallowed by wicked seeds of the enemy in the name of Jesus
3. Dream killers assigned against me die in the name of Jesus.
4. Anointing killers assigned against me die in the name of Jesus
5. Success killers assigned against me die in the name of Jesus
6. Any agent of darkness sowing seed of dream and forget in my life die in the name of Jesus
7. Evil seeds planted in my life die in the name of Jesus.
8. Household wickedness assigned to pull me down meet double failure in the name of Jesus

9. O Lord, convert laughter of powers sowing evil seed in my life to sorrow in the name of Jesus.
10. I break every covenant of evil seeds sowed in my body in the name of Jesus.
11. Let all evil patterns caused by evil seeds be cancelled in the name of Jesus.
12. Every wind of darkness giving helping hands to dream failure, stop by fire in the name of Jesus.
13. Seeds of darkness wither and die in the name of Jesus
14. Troubles emanating from evil plantations expire now in the name of Jesus
15. Every hardship introduced into my life as a result of evil plantation die, in the name of Jesus
16. Rain of fire; fall upon the wicked in the name of Jesus.
17. Every adversary I face as a result of evil seed expires now in the name of Jesus.
18. Lord Jesus nullify every charge brought against me in the kingdom of darkness in the name of Jesus.
19. Thou evil seeds causing blackout in my memory wither and die in the name of Jesus.
20. Thou satanic regulator, regulating my destiny die in the name of Jesus.

PRAYER TO REMEMBER DREAMS

LIBERTY PRAYER NUMBER NINE

EVERY WICKED CURSE SHALL BACKFIRE.

"No weapon that is formed against thee shall prosper, and every tongue that shall rise against thee in judgment thou shalt condemn. This is the heritage of the servants of the LORD, and their righteousness is of me, saith the LORD"
Isaiah 54:17.

PRAYER POINTS

1. Every witchdoctor using the night to trouble me die in the name of Jesus
2. Any evil power assign to curse my memory summersault and die in the name of Jesus
3. Every curse pronounced against my destiny backfire in the name of Jesus
4. Any power pouring libation of darkness against me die in the name of Jesus
5. Every curse that entered me through sleep be purged by the blood of Jesus.
6. Thou trap of darkness assigned against my dream life, catch fire and burn to ashes in the name of Jesus.
7. Any power or personality that is happy because I am not happy, O Lord anoints them with madness in the name of Jesus.

8. Any power making life difficult for me, you are a blood, liar release me by fire in the name of Jesus.
9. Every chain of hardship in my life break to pieces in the name of Jesus.
10. Thou curse of, "You shall dream no more" break in the name of Jesus.
11. Any power that mark me for dream failure, you are a liar, therefore harvest failure in the name of Jesus
12. Every evil sacrifice fashioned against me backfire in the name of Jesus
13. Every power speaking against my destiny shut up and meet failure in the name of Jesus.
14. Every incantation spoken to the heavenly in order to destroy my dream life backfire in the name of Jesus.
15. Any man or woman attacking my star, meet double failure in the name of Jesus
16. Any calabash of darkness assigned against my dream life break into pieces and roast to ashes in the name of Jesus.
17. Any curse pronounced to bury my destiny backfire in the name of Jesus
18. Any power assigned to scatter my destiny you are a failure die in the name of Jesus
19. Every tongue assigned to pull me down wither in the name of Jesus
20. Satanic gang up against my destiny scatter in the name of Jesus.

PRAYER TO REMEMBER DREAMS

LIBERTY PRAYER NUMBER TEN

WICKED BARBERS SHALL DIE

It is written, "Every plant that my heavenly father has not planted will be pulled up by the roots" Mathew 15:13.

PRAYER POINTS

1. Any power assigned to corrupt my dreams die in the name of Jesus.
2. My source of dream shall not dry in the name of Jesus
3. Every wicked agreement assigned to terminate my dream life catch fire in the name of Jesus
4. Every uproar of the enemy against my dream life expire now in the name of Jesus
5. Every threat against me in the dream meet double failure in the name of Jesus
6. My careless attitude that invited spirit barbers into my life expire today in the name of Jesus
7. My life, separate yourself from dream failure in the name of Jesus
8. Morning grief as a result of dream failure expire today in the name of Jesus
9. Thou enemies of my dream, receive arrow of death in the name of Jesus
10. My father, my father, disgrace dream failure in the name of Jesus

11. My father, my father, lift me above dream failure in the name of Jesus
12. I pulled to the root every evil plantation planted in my memory by wicked barbers in the name of Jesus
13. Every wicked instrument of dark barbers assigned to pollute my dream life catch fire and roast to ashes in the name of Jesus.
14. Wicked barbers in charge of my case go blind in the name of Jesus.
15. My lost glory as a result of evil barbers, be restored hundred fold in the name of Jesus
16. Thou dream criminal in charge of my case die in the name of Jesus
17. Any power assigned to waste my dream life die in the name of Jesus
18. Any power that need to die, for my dream to appear and stay, what are you waiting for, die in the name of Jesus.
19. Any power that must die, for my dream to have meanings to me, enough is enough; die now in the name of Jesus.
20. Any power that need to run mad, for me to experience dream and remember power, run mad and die in the name of Jesus.

PRAYER TO REMEMBER DREAMS

LIBERTY PRAYER NUMBER ELEVEN

LAYING ON OF EVIL HANDS SHALL EXPIRE.

"And I will deliver thee out of the hand of the wicked, and I will deliver thee out of the hand of the terrible"
Jeremiah 15:21.

PRAYER POINTS

1. Any power or personalities that laid evil hands upon me in the spirit to scatter my destiny die in the name of Jesus.
2. I cut off every hand of darkness fashioned against my dream life in the name of Jesus.
3. Program of dream failure against my life scatter in the name of Jesus
4. Bad signals in my sleep die in the name of Jesus.
5. Every voice of darkness diverting my dream elsewhere stop by fire in the name of Jesus
6. By the power of resurrection, I convert dry dreams to streams of dreams and vision in the name of Jesus
7. By the power of resurrection I plug my life into the current of dream and remember in the name of Jesus
8. O Lord arise and renew my dream life in the name of Jesus.

9. By the power of resurrection I speak life into my memory bank in the name of Jesus.
10. By the power of resurrection I bind dream killers assigned against me in the name of Jesus.
11. By the power of resurrection, let every destructive hands laid upon my head wither in the name of Jesus
12. By the power of resurrection, I recover what I lost as a result of laying of evil hands upon me in the name of Jesus.
13. By the power of resurrection, let any good thing that died as a result of evil laying of hands receive life now.
14. Yoke of evil hands upon my life, break in the name of Jesus
15. Satanic influence as a result of laying of evil hands upon my life scatter in the name of Jesus.
16. I come against evil judgment to paralyse my dream lie in the name of Jesus.
17. I counter every laying of evil hands upon me with anointing of God in the name of Jesus.
18. O Lord, arise, and let my destiny change in the name of Jesus
19. Holy Ghost Power, padlock the mouth of the enemy against my destiny in the name of Jesus.
20. Reverses assigned for me, as a result of laying on of evil hands upon me shall

PRAYER TO REMEMBER DREAMS

expire, and be converted to signs and wonders in my life in the name of Jesus.

LIBERTY PRAYER NUMBER TWELVE

WICKED ARROWS SHALL BACKFIRE.

"Contend, O LORD, with those who contend with me, fight against those who fight against me" Psalm 35:1.

NOW SING THIS SONG
EVIL ARROW GO BACK TO YOUR SENDER
EVIL ARROW GO BACK TO YOUR SENDER

PRAYER POINTS

1. Every arrow of dream and forget fired against me backfire in the name of Jesus
2. Arrow of memory loss fired against me backfire in the name of Jesus
3. Every form of arrow of wickedness fired against me backfire in the name of Jesus
4. Every arrow fired to cause blackout in my brain backfire in the name of Jesus
5. Sad experience of dream and forget caused as a result of evil arrow end now in the name of Jesus.
6. Wicked arrow fired against my dream life backfire in the name of Jesus
7. Arrow of forgetfulness fired against me backfire in the name of Jesus

PRAYER TO REMEMBER DREAMS

8. I fire back all satanic arrows keeping me in the valley of blackout in the name of Jesus
9. Arrow of dream failure fired against me backfire in the name of Jesus
10. Every wind of affliction against my dream, stop by fire in the name of Jesus
11. Every arrow of oppression, be lifted away by fire in the name of Jesus
12. Arrow of spiritual blindness fired against me backfire, in the name of Jesus
13. Every affliction as a result of wicked arrows backfire in the name of Jesus
14. Every arrow fired against me causing unbelief on dream die in the name of Jesus.
15. My dream life, receive divine healing in the name of Jesus
16. I recover from shocks of wicked arrow in the name of Jesus
17. My destiny shall not be polluted as a result of wicked arrow in the name of Jesus
18. Every yoke of limitation caused by arrow of darkness shall die in the name of Jesus
19. Every hardship introduced into my life as a result of evil arrow shall expire and die in the name of Jesus
20. Set backs introduced into my life by evil arrow shall become my set up for dream breakthrough in the name of Jesus.

LIBERTY PRAYER NUMBER THIRTEEN

I SHALL EAT NO MORE IN THE DREAM.

"And I will deliver thee out of the hand of the wicked, and I will redeem thee out of the hand of the terrible".
Jeremiah 15:21.

PRAYER POINTS

1. Every evil hand, feeding me in the dream in order to steal my dream memory wither in the name of Jesus
2. Every dark agent that fed me in the dream and cause me to forget my dreams after sleep die in the name of Jesus.
3. Every food I ate in the dream assigned to turn me useless in dream kingdom; I purge you by the blood of Jesus
4. Every food I ate in the dream now troubling my retentive memory die in the name of Jesus
5. Every dream sponsored by dark powers to destroy my dream die in the name of Jesus.
6. Every strongman or women behind my eating in the dream die in the name of Jesus
7. I reverse every evil dream walking against my matching forward in the name of Jesus

PRAYER TO REMEMBER DREAMS

8. Every problem that entered me through eating in the dream die in the name of Jesus
9. Every caterer of darkness assigned to cook my food in the spirit, die in the name of Jesus
10. Every messenger of darkness assigned to feed me in the dream, die on your way in the name of Jesus
11. I recover my lost glory as a result of eating in the dream.
12. I recover my dream life polluted as a result of eating in the dream.
13. As from today, I shall eat no more in the dream, in the name of Jesus.
14. Blood of Jesus, purge every poison in my body in the name of Jesus.
15. My dream life, come back with meanings in the name of Jesus.
16. Every arrow fired against me as a result of eating in the dream backfire in the name of Jesus
17. Every wickedness targeted against me by powers of darkness, backfire in the name of Jesus.
18. O God, make my dream life manifest by fire in the name of Jesus.
19. I shall arise and shine, in the name of Jesus.
20. O Lord, quicken my dream life now in the name of Jesus.

LIBERTY PRAYER NUMBER FOURTEEN

I SHALL NOT BE PRESSED DOWN.

It is written, ***"From henceforth let no man trouble me: For I bear in my body the marks of the Lord Jesus"***
Galatians 6:17.

PRAYER POINTS

1. O Lord, crush every oppressor assign to oppress me in the dream, in the name of Jesus.
2. As no one can hinder the glory of the moon, my dream shall appear by fire in the name of Jesus
3. Agents of oppressions assigned against me stumble and die in the name of Jesus
4. Any power operating against my dream life die in the name of Jesus
5. Every idol pressing me down in the sleep die in the name of Jesus
6. Masquerades in charge of my case catch fire and roast to ashes in the name of Jesus.
7. Every strategy of the enemy against my soul scatter in the name of Jesus.
8. Hidden household wickedness that expose me to easy attack die in the name of Jesus.

PRAYER TO REMEMBER DREAMS

9. I recover all I lost as a result of being pressed down in the dream in the name of Jesus.
10. Agenda of darkness against my soul scatter in the name of Jesus
11. You powers that refuse to let me go, die and rise no more in the name of Jesus
12. Thou rod of affliction placed on me in the dream be lifted and die in the name of Jesus
13. Oh my soul, refuse to obey instructions of the enemy in the name of Jesus
14. I refuse to be oppressed or disgraced by dark powers in the name of Jesus.
15. I refuse to be taken captive by dark powers in the name of Jesus
16. I plug myself to Holy Ghost Power therefore, any power that press me down shall die in the name of Jesus.
17. Any power on assignment to press me down die on your way in the name of Jesus.
18. I cancel consequences of being pressed in the dream in the name of Jesus.
19. Spirit of delay and backwardness caused as a result of being pressed down in the dream expire, in the name of Jesus.
20. Holy Ghost, equip me with sword to kill powers assigned to press me down in the name of Jesus

LIBERTY PRAYER NUMBER FIFTEEN

I COME AGAINST SEX IN THE DREAM.

"For we wrestle not against flesh and blood, but against principalities, against powers, against the rulers of the darkness of this world, against spiritual wickedness in high places"
Ephesians 6:12.

PRAYER POINTS

1. I come against spirit spouse tormenting my dream life in the name of Jesus.
2. Any power or personalities that turn my bed to palace of immorality go blind and die in the name of Jesus.
3. Any power messing me up in the dream die in the name of Jesus.
4. All demonically organized seductive appearance in my dream expire in the name of Jesus.
5. Lust of flesh in my body; die in the name of Jesus.
6. Spiritual remote control against my spirit, die in the name of Jesus.
7. Every problem that entered me through sex in the dream die in the name of Jesus.
8. Sex harassment against me in the dream come to an end today in the name of Jesus.

PRAYER TO REMEMBER DREAMS

9. Thou gifts in the physical, manifesting spirit spouse in my life, catch fire and roast to ashes in the name of Jesus.
10. Every spiritual wickedness in high places controlling the affairs of my life die in the name of Jesus.
11. Thou rulers of darkness of this world, my life is not your candidate, therefore leave me alone and die in the name of Jesus.
12. I am released from the grip of principalities and powers, in the name of Jesus.
13. Any power in charge of my dream, become powerless and die in the name of Jesus.
14. O Lord, save me from side effects of sex in the dream.
15. I immunize my doors, windows, roofs, walls and every entrance into my house with blood of Jesus.
16. I break every conscious and unconscious covenant with spirit spouse in the name of Jesus.
17. Every dream blackout caused by sex in the dream come to an end now in the name of Jesus.
18. Every blackout agenda for my life expire today by fire in the name of Jesus.
19. Winds of affliction against my dream backfire in the name of Jesus.
20. My blessings and miracles which I lost as a result of sex in the dream, I recover you back by fire in the name of Jesus.

LIBERTY PRAYER NUMBER SIXTEEN

DREAM BLACKOUT IN MY LIFE SHALL EXPIRE.

"Don't be afraid", the prophet answered. "Those who are with us are more than those who are with them"
2 kings 6:16.

PRAYER POINTS

1. O Lord, with your blood search for my dreams and restore it by fire in the name of Jesus.
2. Owner of evil load in my memory bank and body carry your evil load in the name of Jesus.
3. Every problem attached to my dream life, melt away in the name of Jesus.
4. Marks of darkness in my body, I wipe you off by the blood of Jesus.
5. Every power blocking heavenly spirit from delivering message to me from the heavenly, die in the name of Jesus.
6. My covenant with dream blackout, break in the name of Jesus.
7. Dream killers in my life die in the name of Jesus.
8. Internal bondage in me die in the name of Jesus.

PRAYER TO REMEMBER DREAMS

9. Holy Ghost Power promote me above dream blackout in the name of Jesus.
10. Any power resisting my star to shine, die in the name of Jesus.
11. Prophecy of darkness against my dream life backfire in the name of Jesus.
12. Holy Ghost Fire, devour evil deposits in my life in the name of Jesus.
13. I overthrow powers of dream failure supervising my life, in the name of Jesus
14. Evil bands, release me, in the name of Jesus.
15. Every evil remote control fashioned against my life, die in the name of Jesus.
16. I delete my name from dream and forget register in the name of Jesus.
17. Agents of spiritual blindness in the corridor of my life die, in the name of Jesus.
18. I come against wasters and emptier of dreams assigned against me in the name of Jesus.
19. Dream erasers against my life die in the name of Jesus.
20. Every negative handwriting against my dream life expire today by fire in the name of Jesus.

TELLA OLAYERI

LIBERTY PRAYER NUMBER SEVENTEEN

MY SOURCE OF SPIRITUAL POWER SHALL NOT DRY.

"Some trust in chariots and some in horses, but we trust in the name of the LORD our God"
Psalm 20:7.

PRAYER POINTS.

1. Anything in me, killing my dream die in the name of Jesus.
2. Key of David, open doors of my dream memory now in the name of Jesus.
3. I refuse to deposit my keys of dream in the valley of emptiness in the name of Jesus.
4. I cancel statements of witchdoctors against my dream life in the name of Jesus.
5. O Lord, give me power to decode my dreams in the name of Jesus.
6. Every arrow fired against my joy backfire in the name of Jesus.
7. Balm of Gilead, go to the source of my dream miracle and heal it in the name of Jesus.
8. O Lord, you never fail, do not allow my dream memory fail in the name of Jesus.

PRAYER TO REMEMBER DREAMS

9. Holy Spirit, help my spirit life, in the name of Jesus.
10. Every midnight battle that caged my dream scatter in the name of Jesus.
11. Thou hosts of darkness assigned against my spiritual elevation, I bring judgment of God against you, in the name of Jesus.
12. Holy Ghost destroy every wickedness planted against the source of my power in the name of Jesus.
13. I refuse to be enslaved in the dream in the name of Jesus.
14. Any pot of darkness assigned to dry my spirit being break to pieces in the name of Jesus.
15. Oh Lord, water every good thing that is dead in my life in the name of Jesus.
16. Every arrow fired at me while I was young; now troubling my dream life, die in the name of Jesus.
17. Thou demon of adversity die in the name of Jesus.
18. Every dark river polluting my dream life dry up by fire in the name of Jesus.
19. Holy Ghost, arrest and kill powers delegated to pull me down in the name of Jesus.
20. My trust in the Lord shall remain permanent in the name of Jesus.

LIBERTY PRAYER NUMBER EIGHTEEN

DREAM DEVOURERS, VOMIT MY DREAMS.

"He hath swallowed down riches, and he shall vomit them up again: God shall cast them out of his belly"
Job 20:15.

PRAYER POINTS

1. Every power that swallowed my dreams vomit them now in the name of Jesus.
2. My memory bank hidden by dark powers receive freedom and locate me in the name of Jesus.
3. Any power that wants to waste my dream life be wasted in the name of Jesus.
4. Thou devourer of my dream, be swallowed by horrible tempest of the Lord.
5. Thou enemy of my dream, my God rebuke you in the name of Jesus.
6. Every agent of the grave assigned to swallow my destiny die in the name of Jesus.
7. Any power using evil pot to fight my destiny die in the name of Jesus.

PRAYER TO REMEMBER DREAMS

8. Every evil tree growing in the garden of my life in order to swallow my dreams be uprooted by fire in the name of Jesus.
9. You evil devourer troubling my sleep, receive sharp sword of God and be silent in the grave, in the name of Jesus.
10. O Lord, rain your fire of anger upon the wicked in the name of Jesus.
11. Holy Ghost, break the backbone of dream devourers assigned against me in the name of Jesus.
12. Dream devourers! I refuse to be your candidate, therefore leave me alone and die, in the name of Jesus.
13. Military angels of the living God, press the stomach of dream devourers to vomit my dreams by fire in the name of Jesus.
14. Strange confusion, take over every power assigned to cause me havoc in the name of Jesus.
15. My potentials in the custody of enemies, turn to fire, escape and locate me in the name of Jesus.
16. Every satanic animal controlling affairs of my dream life summersault and die in the name of Jesus.

17. Witchcraft presence in my dream, enough is enough expire and rise no more in the name of Jesus.
18. Mirror of darkness used in monitoring my sleep, break in the name of Jesus.
19. Every desire of the enemy against my life shall meet double failure in the name of Jesus.
20. Every affliction introduced into my life by dream devourers release me and die in the name of Jesus.

PRAYER TO REMEMBER DREAMS

LIBERTY PRAYER NUMBER NINETEEN

EVIL POWERS SHALL NOT LIMIT MY DREAM

"I have given you authority to trample on snakes and scorpions and to overcome all the power of the enemy, nothing will harm you"
Luke 10:19.

PRAYER POINTS

1. Any power that say I shall dream no more, you are a liar die in the name of Jesus.
2. Every padlock of darkness assigned against my dream life break and scatter in the name of Jesus.
3. Every environmental witchcraft power, gathered against my dream life, scatter in the name of Jesus.
4. My laughter that suddenly seize as a result of dream attacks, come back by fire, in the name of Jesus.
5. Every court of darkness challenging my dream life, I set you ablaze, catch fire and roast to ashes in the name of Jesus.
6. Thou strongman behind my dream predicaments, summersault and die, in the name of Jesus.
7. Every gate of sorrow holding me captive, catch fire and roast to ashes in the name of Jesus.

8. Wicked decision taken against me in the spirit scatter in the name of Jesus.
9. Any power in my habitation that wants my glory to sink you are a failure, die in the name of Jesus.
10. Any sickness planted in my life, today is your last day, die in the name of Jesus.
11. Every instrument of darkness assigned against my sleep die in the name of Jesus.
12. Every ancient shrine holding my dream in captivity catch fire and roast to ashes in the name of Jesus.
13. Every agent of dream killer living in my body die in the name of Jesus.
14. I reject dream failure in my life in the name of Jesus.
15. I cast spirit of dream failure out of my life in the name of Jesus.
16. Every evil bird assigned to swallow my dream fall down and die in the name of Jesus.
17. Holy Ghost, destroy every strength that give enemies edge over me in the name of Jesus.
18. Every seed of limitation in me die, in the name of Jesus.
19. Every wicked prayer against my spiritual growth, scatter in the name of Jesus.
20. O Lord, apply divine salt of life into my memory bank for dream manifestation in the name of Jesus.

PRAYER TO REMEMBER DREAMS

LIBERTY PRAYER NUMBER TWENTY

I TOUCH THE GARMENT OF JESUS.

"We have escaped like a bird out of the fowler's snare; the snare has been broken, and we have escaped"
Psalm 124:7.

PRAYER POINTS

1. I touch the garment of Jesus, and remember my dreams by fire in the name of Jesus.
2. I touch the garment of Jesus, my spirit escaped like a bird out of the fowler's snare.
3. I touch the garment of Jesus; dream blackout vanished from my life in the name of Jesus.
4. I touch the garment of Jesus, every snare assigned against me break in pieces by fire in the name of Jesus.
5. I touch the garment of Jesus, and receive instant deliverance from dream problems in the name of Jesus.
6. I touch the garment of Jesus, and become victorious in my sleep in the name of Jesus.
7. I touch the garment of Jesus; laughter filled my mouth in the name of Jesus.

8. I touch the garment of Jesus, and receive power to remember my dreams in the name of Jesus.
9. I touch the garment of Jesus, and receive divine conversion unto the Lord in the name of Jesus.
10. I touch the garment of Jesus and become liberated from nightmares in the name of Jesus.
11. I touch the garment of Jesus; I ate no more in the dream in the name of Jesus.
12. I touch the garment of Jesus, sex in the dream disappeared in my life in the name of Jesus.
13. I touch the garment of Jesus, and become spiritually filled with Holy Spirit in the name of Jesus.
14. O Lord, my father, I need a change answer me by fire, in the name of Jesus.
15. I pull off every contrary garment in my body, in the name of Jesus.
16. My expectation of dream and remember shall come to pass today, I shall not write myself off in the name of Jesus.
17. I touch the garment of Jesus, and I vomit dark poisons troubling my soul in the name of Jesus.
18. I touch the garment of Jesus, and retrieve my blessings from the camp of enemy in the name of Jesus

PRAYER TO REMEMBER DREAMS

19. I touch the garment of Jesus, drinkers of blood fled from me in the name Jesus.
20. I touch the garment of Jesus, and receive divine healing in every area of my life in Jesus name I pray. Amen.

LIBERTY PRAYER NUMBER TWENTY-ONE

I SHALL DREAM AND REMEMBER.

"Then shalt thou walk in thy way safely, and thy foot shall not stumble"
Proverbs 3:23.

PRAYER POINTS

1. My memory bank come alive and reveal my dreams to me in the name of Jesus.
2. I shall dream to remember them all in the name of Jesus.
3. O God arise, and let my dream be permanent in the name of Jesus.
4. I release myself from bondage of dream failure in the name of Jesus
5. Holy Ghost Power, blow wind of resurrection upon my dream life in the name of Jesus
6. You evil stranger, keeping vigil to destroy my dream life, die in your duty post in the name of Jesus.
7. I cast spirit of forgetfulness out of my life in the name of Jesus.
8. Any thing that weakens the brain, residing in my life die in the name of Jesus

PRAYER TO REMEMBER DREAMS

9. Any power, boasting I shall remember my dreams no more die with your boast in the name of Jesus.
10. Divine healing from above arrest and restore my dream power to me now in the name of Jesus.
11. When I dream, I shall remember my dream in the name of Jesus.
12. Every dark veil in my brain disappear in the name of Jesus.
13. O Lord, I shall not rest until I dream and remember all, therefore answer me by fire in the name of Jesus.
14. Every priest of evil altar, holding on to the key of my dream, release my key to me now in the name of Jesus.
15. O Lord, let my dream failure go into captivity, in the name of Jesus
16. O Lord, provoke favor on my behalf in the name of Jesus.
17. Affliction shall not rise the second time in my life in the name of Jesus.
18. I am loaded with dream and remember in the name of Jesus.
19. O Lord, deposit seeds of wonders in me that will resurrect my dreams in the name of Jesus.
20. Every hindrance against my dream bank shall die in the name of Jesus.

LIBERTY PRAYER NUMBER TWENTY-TWO

O LORD, SHINE LIGHT OF UNDERSTANDING UPON MY LIFE

"Rejoice not against me, O mine enemy when I fall, I shall arise, when I sit in darkness, the LORD shall be a light unto me"
Micah 7:8.

PRAYER POINTS

1. Light of God, shine on every darkness troubling my spirit being in the name of Jesus.
2. Lord Jesus, incubate me with dreams that will promote my life in the name of Jesus.
3. Lord Jesus visit my soul and shine your resurrection light upon me in the name of Jesus.
4. Light of God, shine and paralyze any power causing dream wastage in my life in the name of Jesus.
5. O Lord, increase your light in my life, in the name of Jesus.
6. O Lord, shine light that will chase darkness out of my life in the name of Jesus.
7. O Lord, make your face shine upon me for signs and wonder in the name of Jesus.

PRAYER TO REMEMBER DREAMS

8. Lord Jesus, shine light upon my path and destiny in the name of Jesus.
9. O Lord, let your light of glory break forth as in the morning upon my destiny in the name of Jesus.
10. Lord Jesus, let your light shine upon me, and heal every form of dream bareness troubling my soul in the name of Jesus.
11. Dream wilderness in my life, bow to light of God in the name of Jesus.
12. Thou light of God, deliver me by fire today and set me free from dream and forget problems in the name of Jesus.
13. O Lord, let your light from heaven destroy every works of darkness holding my dream life in bondage in the name of Jesus.
14. O Lord, let your light shine upon my heart for spiritual revival and dream resurrection.
15. O Lord, revive my heart and let me recognize signs you speak with me in the name of Jesus.
16. O Lord, let your light cleanse me by fire in the name of Jesus.
17. Light of God; kill every stubborn spirit dwelling in my system in the name of Jesus.
18. Lord Jesus, let your light descend upon my enemies like thunder and fire in the name of Jesus.
19. My habitation, open wide and receive light of God in the name of Jesus.

20. Wasting powers of dreams assigned against me, be wasted by light of God.

PRAYER TO REMEMBER DREAMS

LIBERTY PRAYER NUMBER TWENTY-THREE

MY MIRACLE IS NOW

For it is written, "And I will restore to you the years that the locust hath eaten, the cankerworm, and the caterpillar, and the palmerworm, my great army which I sent among you"
Joel 2:25.

PRAYER POINTS

1. Every garment in my life chasing miracles away from me catch fire and roast to ashes in the name of Jesus.
2. O Lord, I am a candidate of miracle dreamers, therefore I convert my good dreams to miracle in the name of Jesus.
3. O Lord, I am a candidate of miracle dreamer, therefore, I reverse every bad dream to miracles in the name of Jesus
4. I hold my staff of strength and claim my dream miracles in the name of Jesus.
5. Dream miracle in my life appear, and experience divine stabilizer that retains dream above witchcraft expectations in the name of Jesus.
6. Lord Jesus, cause positive explosion of greatness in my life in the name of Jesus.

7. Spiritual institutions in the heavenly see to my dream life in the name of Jesus.
8. I proclaim spiritual revival and sound mind to manage my dream world in the name of Jesus.
9. I decree dream miracle and restoration upon my life in the name of Jesus.
10. Lord Jesus, touch my life for miracles today in the name of Jesus.
11. O Lord, meet me in a powerful way to experience miracles in my dream in the name of Jesus.
12. O Lord, transform my life by fire today and let me remember my dreams one after the other in the name of Jesus.
13. O Lord, answer me with revival miracle in the name of Jesus.
14. O Lord, perfect your miracle in my dream life in the name of Jesus.
15. Oh spirit of miracle, open treasures of dreams to me today in the name of Jesus.
16. O Lord, broaden my memory bank with dreams, in the name of Jesus.
17. Divine power of God; fall upon my dream life in the name of Jesus.
18. My father and my God, pull me out of darkness with your miracle hands in the name of Jesus.
19. I command miracles into my life today in the name of Jesus.

20. Witchcraft merchants against my dream life die in the name of Jesus.

SING THIS SONG LOUD AND CLEAR
**MY MIRACLE, MY MIRACLE HAVE STARTED
MY MIRACLE, MY MIRACLE HAVE STARTED
CONCERNING MY DREAMS OOOO
MY MIRACLE HAVE STARTED
MY MIRACLE HAVE STARTED.**

LIBERTY PRAYER NUMBER TWENTY-FOUR

I CLAIM GOOD EXPECTATIONS.

"And the Lord shall deliver me from every evil work, and will preserve me unto his heavenly Kingdom: to whom be glory for ever and ever". Amen
2 Timothy 4:18.

PRAYER POINTS.

1. Grace of the Most High God overshadow my life in the name of Jesus
2. My father, my father, turn me around for dream breakthrough in the name of Jesus
3. This is my season of laughter; it shall not be polluted in the name of Jesus
4. Dream mourning in my life, be converted to dream and recollect in the name of Jesus.
5. Scarcity of testimony in my sleep, today is your last day, be converted to flows of good dreams now in the name of Jesus.
6. I dedicate my dream life to God for signs and wonders in the name of Jesus
7. O Lord, over answer my prayer for dream retention in the name of Jesus
8. I free myself by the power of the Almighty, from dream captivity in the name of Jesus.
9. I claim my dream bank held in bondage in the kingdom of darkness in the name of Jesus.

PRAYER TO REMEMBER DREAMS

10. My good dreams that passed me by, come back, and locate me, in the name of Jesus.
11. Every dream wilderness, having good time in my life, expire in the name of Jesus
12. I overcome every dream amputation fashioned against me in the name of Jesus
13. My warfare against dream failure shall be successful in the name of Jesus
14. My divine spiritual assignments shall not be terminated in the name of Jesus.
15. I claim positive growth of dream wonders in the name of Jesus.
16. Messages in my dreams shall escape no more, in the name of Jesus.
17. My memory bank improve by fire in the name of Jesus.
18. I claim victory over dream failure in the name of Jesus.
19. I claim victory over familiar spirit troubling my dream life in the name of Jesus
20. I claim victory over every form of stronghold holding me captive in the name of Jesus.

CHAPTER TEN.

NINETY-NINE DECREES.

Prayers under decree are divided into three phases:-
1. **Lamentations and Petition 1-30**
2. **Warfare and Battles   31-77**
3. **Confessions and Possessions 78-99**

Cry to God for dream fulfillment. Call upon Him to feed you with heavenly food in your sleep. He sees the future before it unfolds itself to us. We only see a day at a time, while our Father in heaven sees all, now and far beyond.

Hence, you need to fight against narrow spiritual visions and weak commitments with God. Arrest every step that makes you wander far away from dream kingdom. Fight hard and experience dreams flowing from heavenly bank of dreams.

Prayer is a paramount key to success. The more you are prayerfully committed, the more you build faith in God. With the prayers here, believe you shall recover from dream failure. The psalmist says, *"The young lions do lack, and suffer hunger: but they that seek the Lord, shall not want any good thing" Psalm 34:10.* God is still in the business of answering prayers. He can't let you

PRAYER TO REMEMBER DREAMS

down. He knows you more than you know yourself. Before you open your mouth, He knows your petitions and answers you accordingly. All you need to do now, is to concentrate in prayer for dream revival and expect positive revelations.

With fresh fire and vigor in you, move forward in prayer and claim your rights by fire. Hence re-dedicate your life to God in holiness and in prayer. Finally, call it quit with anti-testimony powers assigned to sink or pollute your dream life. Enough is enough.

Your prayer tonight shall involve application of anointing oil on your head, eyes and mouth as directed below. I plead you buy small bottle of anointing oil for this purpose. Follow the instructions as given and expect miracles forthwith. As soon as you pray on the anointing oil, place it safely on one side and continue with your prayer. Thereafter, you shall go into decrees of Psalms and pray the prayers.

STEP ONE: - Pick your anointing oil, raise it to the heavenly and pray like this:-

OPENING PRAYER

O Lord. I raise this anointing oil unto you for signs and wonders in respect of my predicaments on dream and forget. Let it meet your eyes for mercy and favor. Let my petitions be accepted before you for power.

Let your fire enter it, let blood of Jesus flow into it. Let powers of deliverance change its content for signs and wonders. Let the oil become sacred and powerful. Let fire of revival take over its functions. Let the anointing oil destroy works of darkness assigned to pollute my destiny and dream life. Let the anointing oil empower me spiritually in the name of Jesus.

You this anointing oil, God has ordained you as my divine multipurpose instrument of connections and power. Therefore I speak unto you to destroy every works of darkness that placed me in bondage. When I say loose, obey me, hence loose every dark veil, rope, tread or whatever means enemies used in binding me spiritually. When I say dissolve and destroy, do it quickly in the name of Jesus. Hence, you shall dissolve and destroy every evil plantation holding me captive in the territory of dream kingdom.

PRAYER TO REMEMBER DREAMS

As I apply this anointing this day, turn me to a heavenly person entirely. After anointing, comes changes in ones life. When Saul's head was anointed, he became a changed person entirely. When David was anointed with horn of oil, the power of God came mightily upon him and he became a changed person. When the sick is anointed (James 5:14), he is revived. Therefore, when I apply this anointing oil on myself, I shall become a changed person in the name of Jesus. My situation shall change for good. My destiny shall change for signs and wonders. Dream blackout shall vacate my life. My dreams shall become clean and clear, unpolluted and never in fragments. Dreams shall flow in my system undisturbed. I shall be the head and not the tail. My spirit man shall not be rubbished by the enemy. Every affliction against my spirit man shall die. As a covenant child, I am free and shall be free indeed. My God is my redeemer, I am redeemed and free for ever, from dream blackout and from the claws of dream erasers. Amen.

As I shall apply this anointing oil, my prayers shall ascend to heaven for signs and wonders. And so, shall it be in Jesus name, Amen.

STEP TWO.
HEAD
Rub your head with the content of anointing oil in your hands as you pray thus:-
PRAYER
My head, you are the symbol of my glory. As I anoint you today, let my glory shine. When Saul's head was anointed his glory shine, when David's head was anointed his life changed for good. Therefore Lord, as I anoint my head today, let your power fall upon me. Turn me to a powerful changed person that shall route out evil deposits from my life and kill every dark power in charge of my case.

My head, receive special anointing from above. Hence, any power assigned against me from the pit of hell shall die in the name of Jesus. Every arrow fired against me shall backfire and consume the sender. My head is sacred, and so, it shall not be rubbished. Any power assigned to torment me shall fail, for it is written, ***"Do not touch my anointed ones, do my prophets no harm"***. Thus, as an anointed child of God, whoever attack me shall not prosper.

My head, I anoint you with heavenly anointing oil to prosper and remain blessed. My God shall fight for you and I shall be a changed person. O Lord, chase every rascal spirit troubling my soul in the dream. Let every contrary deposit on my head die.

PRAYER TO REMEMBER DREAMS

Let all veils of darkness on my head catch fire. Let my memory bank become fresh. Let every consequence of laying of evil hands upon my head and every arrow of darkness fired against my person backfire. What I lost as a result of evil arrow I recover back by fire.

Anointing that makes one a changed person fall upon me in the name of Jesus. O Lord, let your power locate me by fire. Let your name find place in my mouth in the dream. Let your power of anointing magnetize dreams to my memory bank. As I anoint my head (anoint it again), let me see visions, let me possess retentive memory, let dream become part of me.

As David rightly said, **"You anoint my head with oil, my cup overflows" Psalm 23:5.** Let this anointing oil bring heavenly blessings, favor and mercy unto me. Let my cup of dreams overflow. Let me experience joy over dream blackout. Empower me to remember what I dream in the name of Jesus. Do this for me, O Lord I pray. Amen.

STEP THREE.
EYES
Anoint your eyes with anointing oil in your hands and pray like this:-

PRAYER
O Lord, I anoint my eyes with this blessed heavenly anointing oil. Let power of vision flow in my eyes. Let power of anointing to see, recognize, and remember dreams fall upon me. Let veils of darkness placed on my face disappear by fire. Empower me to recover my spiritual eye glasses in the hands of the enemy. Let every laying of evil hands that affects my vision expire by fire today. Let every spirit of blindness that holds me captive die. As from today, I shall dream, see, and remember my dreams by fire, in the name of Jesus. Amen.

STEP FOUR.

MOUTH

Allow the drops of anointing oil into your mouth. Swallow it and place the bottle safely in a place and pray like this:-

PRAYER

I swallow this heavenly anointing oil into my body system for signs and wonders. O Lord, as the anointing oil pass through my mouth and throat down to my abdomen, let miracles happen in my life. Let deliverance follow suit. Let all contrary deposits in me die. Let powers that swallow dreams and testimonies vacate my life and die. Let evil stores that conceal my dreams in me be pulled down. Let evil plantations in the garden of my life die. Let all conscious and unconscious covenants troubling my spiritual life break. Let distress and afflictions working against my dream life expire today. Let every dream calamity in my life die, in Jesus name I pray, Amen.

STEP FIVE.
BEDDINGS AND WARDROBES
Anoint your beddings and wardrobes with the fresh powerful anointing oil in your hands as you pray like this:-

PRAYER
You this anointing oil in my hands, I apply you upon my beddings and wardrobes. Let fire in you kill every dark agent dwelling in you. Let blood of Jesus inside this anointing oil paralyze and destroy every works of agents of darkness dwelling in my beddings and wardrobes. Blood of Jesus, paralyze their activities by fire. Let every evil plantation dwelling in you die to the root. Let Holy Ghost Power, take over your place. Let powers assigned to paralyze my dream die, in the name of Jesus I pray, Amen.

Fresh anointing of God, take over my beddings and wardrobes. O Lord, as I do this today, let me remember my dreams. Let my beddings and wardrobe become holy and acceptable before you. Let all contrary powers dwelling in them vacate by fire. Let your angels dwell in my habitation relay my dreams to me.
Hence I declare as follows, I shall dream and remember my dreams. My beddings and wardrobes are declared holy. Every contrary power dwelling in my habitation shall die, never to rise again, Amen.

STEP SIX
DOOR ENTRANCE, WINDOWS AND WALLS

Now apply the anointing oil on your door entrance, windows, walls etc and pray like this:-

PRAYER

As I apply this anointing oil on my door entrance, windows, and walls of my house, let power of God take over my dwelling. Let powers that dwell in this anointing oil perform wonders in my habitation. Holy Ghost Power, turn every door of my house to doors of fire, my windows to windows of fire, walls in my house, to walls of fire and roofs in my house to roofs of fire. Let divine fire of God consume every contrary power residing in you. Let every contrary power assigned to disturb my dream life be barricaded by fire.

O God, destroy every satanic door, gates, windows, walls and roofs co-operating with enemies against my life. Overthrow and kill strange powers taking charge of them. Rout out every ancient door, gates and windows in my habitation.

Therefore, let every ancient door and windows assigned to barricade my angels of blessing from visiting me in the dream catch fire and roast to ashes. Thou ancient gates and doors you are condemned already. Hear what the book of Psalms say, obey it by fire.

7 "Lift up your heads, O you gates
Be lifted up, you ancient doors,
That the King of glory may come in

8 "Who is this King of glory?.
The LORD strong and mighty,
The LORD mighty in battle.

9. Lift up your heads, O you gates,
Lift them up, you ancient doors,
That the King of glory may come in,

10. Who is this King of glory?
The LORD Almighty-
he is the King of glory"
Psalm 24:7-10.

Henceforth, all ancient doors and gates troubling my soul shall bow and die in the name of Jesus. Angels of Living God visit my sleep unhindered. Thou heaven, announce obituary of contrary powers causing blockage against angels of God from visiting me. Let fire of God chase every contrary power in my habitation, for my house is inhabited with fire of Holy Ghost.

Thou dark agent outside my house I barricade you by fire. Hence, my entrance shall become consuming fire before you. Anyone that prove to be stubborn among you, fire of God shall paralyze,

PRAYER TO REMEMBER DREAMS

blindfold and break your wings in the name of Jesus. Therefore, you shall operate no more in my vicinity, in the name of Jesus Amen.

Henceforth, my habitation is declared holy, and shall remain holy, for ever and ever, Amen.

STEP SEVEN.
THANKSGIVING
Give thanks to the Almighty God, for what he has done tonight.

I thank you Lord, for the prayers so far. I thank you Lord, as you shall usher me into decrees of the books of Psalms, I shall pray next. I thank you Lord, after praying this prayer you shall restore my dream memory to enable me dream and remember my dreams to the letter. Amen.

Now go to the next prayer session and pray through all prayers of decrees in the next chapter.

PRAYER TO REMEMBER DREAMS

DECREES, USING THE BOOKS OF PSALMS

LAMENTATIONS AND PETITIONS

DECREE NUMBER ONE

"If you, O LORD, kept a record of sins, O LORD, who could stand? But with you there is forgiveness, therefore you are feared"
Psalm 130:3-4.

O Lord, I am a sinner, my cup overflows with sin. I am a person of multiple sins. In my mother's womb, I am a sinner, because by biological parents are sinners. I fed on what they ate while I was in the womb. When I was put to bed, I was welcome into this sinful earth by sinners. Thereafter, when I knew what is good from bad, I took side with sinful acts. This qualifies me a sinner before the Lord.

O Lord, if you kept a record of sins, I am not qualify to open my mouth before you. Your holiness is incomparable. Your majesty is unpolluted. Your hands are clean. I cry unto you for forgiveness and power to resist sin. My sins led to dream predicaments in my life. Dream blackout ravaged my life. I forget my dreams so easily, where I remember them, it is in fragments.

O Lord, I call upon you for the forgiveness of my sins and the resurrection of my dream in the name of Jesus. Amen.

PRAYER TO REMEMBER DREAMS

DECREE NUMBER TWO

"He is like a tree planted by streams of water, which yields its fruit in season and whose leaf does not wither. Whatever he does prosper"
Psalm 1:3.

Father Lord, you created me for excellence, and by your grace to yield and harvest my labor bountifully. You created me for fruitfulness, but my spirit in the dream is hurt by agents of darkness. I hardly remember my dreams any more. My sleep timetable is polluted. My spiritual connection is under attack. I am but a struggler in the territory of dream kingdom. Hence, I call upon you to free me from wilderness of sleep blackout. O Lord help me out. Let me recover my dream life by your magnetic power. Let powers and magnets to remember dreams dwell in my brain.

I decree streams of divine water of resurrection to operate in my life. I decree your presence into my life. I decree power of dream and remember to locate me by fire and command my dreams to yield fruitful results. Hence, I curse every spirit of dryness in me to die, for ever and ever, Amen.

DECREE NUMBER THREE.

"He brought them out of darkness and the deepest gloom and broke away their chains" Psalm 107:14.

O Lord, save me from power of darkness. Break chains of darkness holding me captive. Clear every forms of power of darkness holding my sleep into ransom. Redeem me from the hands of my foes. Let my hunger to remember my dreams receive answer. Let era of dream and forget in my life be a thing of past. Bring to an end every form of storm assigned against my dreams. Exalt me O Lord in the presence of my enemies. Save me from sleep distress. Let smiles of joy find place in my face. Heal me of wounds inflicted on me by enemies. Scatter the plans of the enemy to enslave me in the dream. Pour anointing of remembrance upon my head.

Hence, I decree wonders into my life. I decree light of God upon my life, to heal and perfect wonders in my dream life, in the name of Jesus. I command thunder fire of God to break every chain of darkness holding me captive. I shall not shake my head in distress as a result of dream failure; neither shall my heart be filled with sorrow after sleep, in Jesus name I pray Amen.

DECREE NUMBER FOUR.

"The LORD is a refuge for the oppressed, a stronghold in times of trouble"
Psalm 9:9.

Who can I call upon in time of trouble? It is Jesus. Here I come before you O Lord; I am oppressed in sleep, in dream and in spirit. I run to you for safety so that you might save me from dream memory loss. Save my soul from jackals that torment me in my sleep. My sleep time table is under serious attack of the wicked. Save me from the oppression of wickedness. O Lord, you are my refuge, save me Lord.

Use your power of decree to save me from dream calamity, dream oppression and dream failure. Hence, I decree liberty and dream breakthrough into my life, now and forevermore, Amen.

DECREE NUMBER FIVE.

"I cry aloud to the LORD, I lift up my voice to the LORD for mercy. I pour out my complaint before him, before him I tell my trouble"
Psalm 142:1-2.

O Lord, I cry loud unto you for mercy. I cry aloud to you for favor and mercy. I cry unto you concerning the troubles I face day in day out. My dream foundation is shaking. Enemies inflict my dream life. I am but a shadow in my sleep, as I remember none of my dream after sleep.

I complain bitterly before people, yet help does not come from them. I wept concerning same, my situation never change. My parents, friends, teachers, pastors and neighbors alike, could not provide answer to it. I look all around, east, south, west and north, yet there is no answer.

Hence, I lift my eyes unto the hills, unto the holy throne, unto the heavenly, where answer can be received. O Lord, decree power of revival to take place in my life. Let your decree from your holy throne bring changes into my life today. Amen.

PRAYER TO REMEMBER DREAMS

DECREE NUMBER SIX.

"I say to God my Rock, "Why have you forgotten me? Why must I go about mourning, oppressed by the enemy?"
Psalm 42:9.

I cancel, and render null and void oppressions of the enemy against my soul. I release my soul from the grip of the enemy. I fire back arrow of spiritual blindness fired at me. I remove and burn to ashes every garment of mourning troubling my soul.

O Lord, dress me with garment of favor and mercy. Forgive me of sins holding me captive; do not allow me to die in this situation. Let your anointing fall upon me, empower me to remember my dreams, in Jesus name I pray Amen.

DECREE NUMBER SEVEN

"Blessed is he whose transgressions are forgiven, whose sins are covered. Blessed is the man whose sin the LORD does not count against him and in whose spirit is no deceit".
Psalm 32:1-2

My sins held me captive, transgressions speak loud against me. In the midst of these, I am entangled in the hands of the enemies. I am brutally cornered from communicating with heaven through dreams. My spiritual liberty is tampered with. To you Oh Lord, I cry unto for forgiveness of sins which stand as legal ground against me before my enemies. Forgive me Lord, save me from spiritual blackout.

Pronounce your decree upon my situation. Decree dream revival upon me, let me remember my dreams. Anoint me afresh and let your decree stand, in the name of Jesus I pray Amen.

DECREE NUMBER EIGHT.

"They spread a net for my feet— I was bowed down in distress. They dug a pit in my path— but they have fallen into it themselves"
Psalm 57:6.

Lord Jesus, rescue me from the hands of dark powers breathing wickedness against my soul. These powers are out for evil. They spread evil nets to capture me in the sleep. They feed me time without number in the dream. Spirit spouse troubled me all night. I was pursued in the dream for destruction. They spread net for my feet, to catch and imprison me. They dug pits along my path, so that I may fall into their traps. All these were done to let me dwell in distress and confusion. They fired arrow of memory loss against me and make me fall prey to them.

Save me Lord, release me from the captivity of the enemy. Let me remember my dreams as in the beginning, as you promised us from your Holy seat. Decree goodness into my life, let liberty reign in my life, in Jesus name I pray Amen. Amen.

DECREE NUMBER NINE.

"Those who hate me without reason outnumber the hairs of my head, many are my enemies without cause——"
Psalm 69:4.

Lord Jesus, enemies surround me, wicked attackers do vigil to pollute my sleep. I am hated without cause. Those who laugh with me in day time suddenly turn to monsters at night to torment me. They destroy and devour messages ascribe for me in the heavenly. I became a mere decorator on my bed. I am trample upon at will. Evil seeds were sowed in me in the dream. I am but a shadow of myself. Anytime people discuss dreams, I become an onlooker because I have nothing to contribute. I forget my dreams before I wake up, sometimes I don't dream at all. I am robbed oh Lord!

Rescue me from the shadow of death. Build me afresh, let my memory bank function well. To you Oh Lord I cry. Amen.

PRAYER TO REMEMBER DREAMS

DECREE NUMBER TEN.

"In your distress you called and I rescued you. I answered you out of a thunder cloud, I tested you at the waters of Meribah."
Psalm 81:7.

I have no other God apart from you O Lord, for you are my God and my Lord. When I called you in my distress, you rescued me, out of your thunder cloud you answered me. I call upon you today to liberate me from powers of dream erasers. They are powers that rob victims of dreams. They introduce blackout into people's memory. Hence, they make one forget dreams, or not to dream at all.

This is my situation now, O Lord rescue me, help me out. Let me dream and remember my dreams. Let me dream and be a conqueror in the spirit. Decree justice against the enemy, decree liberty upon my life, in Jesus name I pray. Amen.

DECREE NUMBER ELEVEN.

"May my prayer be set before you like incense, may the lifting up of my hands be like the evening sacrifice"
Psalm 141:2.

O Lord, I call on you this day for signs and wonders, come quickly to me, answer me by fire. Hear my prayer as I stretch my hands of prayer to you. Listen to my cry for mercy, redeem my dream life. I dream and forget all, sometimes I remember just few. These robbed me spiritual matters. I live far from heavenly message. I am no more connected in the dream realm. This is my lamentation before you. O Lord, save me from the hand of dream failure and dream pollution caused by whirlwind of darkness.

I lift up my hands unto you for answer. May the lift of my hands be like the evening sacrifice, ready for an answer. I shall receive answer to dream and forget problems facing me today. Let my dream life experience spiritual revival. Let every dark power and personal contributions that led to dream failure in my life come to an end today. Therefore, I nullify sad effects against my dream life, and experience explosive turnaround from dream and forget, to dream and remember.

PRAYER TO REMEMBER DREAMS

O God, do this speedily, I know you shall do it, Amen.

DECREE NUMBER TWELVE.

"Listen to my prayer, O God, do not ignore my plea".
Psalm 55:1.

O Lord my father, hear my prayer, listen to the words of my mouth. Do not look at my deeds for I am but a sinner. Have mercy on me; wash me clean of my sins. Enemies robbed me of good things and trample upon me. I hardly dream, and when I'm opportune to dream, I forget them all. As a result, my heart is filled with anguish, happiness found no place in me when I wake from sleep.

O Lord, deliver me from dream oppressors, and powers assigned to devour me of my dreams. Let your heavenly decree set me free. Let liberty reign in my life. Amen.

DECREE NUMBER THIRTEEN.

"My tears have been my food day and night, while men say to me all day long, "Where is your God"
Psalm 42: 3.

Lord Jesus, I am filled with soberness, tears rolled down my cheeks. Whenever I realize, I can't remember my dreams after sleep, I felt bad. Going to bed at night is like a dead man going to sleep. On my bed, I do not dream, even when I dream I forget all. This made tears become my food day and night. My heart is depressed and full of sorrow. Arise, O Lord, help me out, and empower me to remember my dreams.

O Lord, lay your hands upon me, to enable me dream and remember what I dream. Open my eyes to see visions. Decree your heavenly power upon my life. Let your mighty power dwell in me. I know you shall do it. Even, my God have done it. I claim victory over dream and forget and so shall it be in Jesus, name Amen.

DECREE NUMBER FOURTEEN.

"I do not trust in my bow, my sword does not bring me victory, but you give us victory over our enemies, you put our adversaries to shame".
Psalm 44:6.

Lord Jesus, I have tried the best I could in respect of my dream life, yet there is no positive result. I cry and wail it was as if I added fuel to fire. Darkness overtook my dream life. I am powerless over my situation. At this junction, I realize it is only you who can save me from predicaments.

Pronounce decree of judgment from above against my foes. Decree dream revival upon my dream life. Decree success and breakthrough upon me. I rely on you Oh Lord, do it speedily. Amen.

PRAYER TO REMEMBER DREAMS

DECREE NUMBER FIFTEEN.

"The voice of the LORD strikes with flashes of lightning. The voice of the LORD shakes the desert; the LORD shakes the Desert of Kadesh". Psalm 29:7-8.

The Lord is enthroned as King forever. His voice represents last command to all. When he speaks peace, it comes to pass. When he speaks war, he takes control. Blessed is my sleep in the name of Jesus. By his power, peace locates me. Flashes of lightning from his mouth strike my enemies down. His support shall make me a champion.

O Lord, let your warfare angels destroy powers causing blackout in my sleep. Let the lamentation of "I dream and forget all", "I dream I cannot remember all", end today. Speak Lord; let your voice strike with flashes of lightning upon my destiny. Cause revival in my memory bank, to enable me remember my dreams clearly. Amen.

DECREE NUMBER SIXTEEN.

"He lies in wait like a lion in cover he lies in wait to catch the helpless, he catches the helpless and drags them off in his net"
Psalm 10:9.

O Lord, enemies are desperate to harm and destroy me in the spirit. They penciled me down as a candidate who has no helper. But you are my helper O Lord.

They caught me in the sleep and cause me to forget my dreams. They rendered me helpless, as I do not know how mightily they deal with me in the dream. The fact is I hardly remember my dreams. They drag me off in their net. They laugh as they do so, asking me, where is my God?

Yes, my safety has come. My God has risen to my situation. He decree freedom into my life and it came to pass. O Lord, I obey your decree, enemies bowed down to it as well. *"Your decrees are the theme of my song wherever I lodge" Psalm 119:54.* Hence, I walk out of evil nets holding me captive. My God decree remembrance into my memory bank.

PRAYER TO REMEMBER DREAMS

DECREE NUMBER SEVENTEEN.

"Why are you down cast, O my soul? Why so disturbed within me? Put your hope in God, for I will yet praise him, my savior and my God.
Psalm 42:5.

My praise goes to my God, the creator of the earth and universe, who sees everything, nothing is hidden from him. He knew my plights. He knew I faintly remember my dreams. At times I forget all! Lord Jesus, before I open my mouth you knew my heart. The fact is I am downcast, Oh Lord, concerning my situation. Help me Lord so that I might remember my dreams. Reverse every evil word spoken against my memory. Anoint me with anointing of dream and recollect. Pull every arrow of forgetfulness out of me.

Treat my case with urgently, let it receive the label "emergency" in the name of Jesus. Hence, I decree success and wonders into my life. My dream and prayer life shall not experience blockage anymore in the name of Jesus. Amen.

DECREE NUMBER EIGHTEEN

"In his arrogance the wicked man hunts down the weak, who are caught in the schemes he devises"
Psalm 10:2.

O Lord the wicked vowed to place me in permanent cloud of dream blackout. Satan and his agents placed me in bad shape of dream captivity. I am weak in dream memory. I lost account of my dreams, I fell prey of his schemes. I ate and have sex in the dream; even my prayer life has diminished.

These and many other reasons made me a prey in the hands of the wicked. I am arrogantly supervised to dream and forget my dreams. Rescue me Lord, let me recover my spiritual power and senses toady. To you O Lord, I pray, Amen.

PRAYER TO REMEMBER DREAMS

DECREE NUMBER NINETEEN.

"As a father has compassion on his children, so the LORD has compassion on those who fear him".
Psalm 103:13.

Lord Jesus, crown me with love and compassion, redeem my life with your precious blood. Your presence in my life drives enemies far away. They ran and never look back. O Lord, let your fear occupy my mind so that I don't miss my step in the walk of life.

Let enemies vanish from the corridor of my life. Endeavor me to sing praises of rejoice of, "I can remember my dreams now". Renew and rebuild my memory. Let every cloud and darkness ruling my sleep vanish. Cover me with your heavenly feather; let me take refuge under your wings. So help me Lord. Amen.

DECREE NUMBER TWENTY.

"Be merciful to me, O LORD, for I am in distress, my eyes grow weak with sorrow, my soul and my body with grief. My life is consumed by anguish and my years by groaning, my strength fails because of my affliction and my bones grow weak".
Psalm 31:9-10.

Lord Jesus, I register my complaints of dream and forget before you this day. My petition concerns blackout arrow fired against my dream memory, causing me distress and sorrow. My strength fails, as I can't remember my dreams which may serve as spiritual guide for my advancement in life. I cry to you this day O Lord, to anoint me afresh to remember my dreams.

Let afflictions flee my life. Let spirit of Joseph of dream and interpret dreams fall upon me for signs and wonders in Jesus name I pray Amen.

PRAYER TO REMEMBER DREAMS

DECREE NUMBER TWENTY-ONE.

"But my eyes are fixed on you, O Sovereign LORD, in you I take refuge do not give me over to death"
Psalm 141:8

To dream and forget, is close to untimely death. Anytime I dream and forget my dreams, I am denied spiritual messages which can make or mar me. Forgetfulness of dreams, mean living in darkness, and when one lives in darkness, he is close to death, untimely death indeed.

This is the position enemies placed me now, because I hardly remember my dreams. But unto you O Lord I fixed my eyes, in you I take refuge. Let me recover from dream and forget. Let my dream life be re-generated for spiritual messages. Engineer my spiritual life to fit in to heavenly realm.

Therefore, I decree remembrance into my dream life. I decree understanding into my heart. I decree salvation into my soul, in the name of Jesus. Amen.

DECREE NUMBER TWENTY-TWO.

"Let the morning bring me word of your unfailing love, for I put my trust in you. Show me the way I should go, for to you I lift up my soul"
Psalm 143:8.

O Lord, let morning gives me joy, happiness and unfailing love from above. Let me wake every morning with hope and joy. Let panic and fears of dream and forget vacate the corridor of my life. Let me wake and remember my dreams. Let every power that snatch dream from my memory paralyze. Let my morning be loaded with testimonies of Hallelujah!

I shall remember my dreams to the letter. I shall harvest dreams of my sleep. My spirit being is alive. My God shall do wonders in my life, and I shall enjoy his unfailing love, forever and ever. Amen.

PRAYER TO REMEMBER DREAMS

DECREE NUMBER TWENTY-THREE.

"Give me a sign of your goodness, that my enemies may see it and be put to shame, for you, O LORD, have helped me and comforted me"
Psalm 86:17.

O Lord, you are my comforter and savior. In my sleep I am troubled and robbed of spiritual right to dream. I want my dream life to resurrect with sound foundation built upon the Rock of Ages. O Lord, give me just a sign of your goodness to remember my dreams and narrate them vividly. Do this O Lord, because the spirit controls the physical.

Save me from been wasted by dark wasters, to you O LORD I cry. Let signs and wonders follow suit in my dream life. Hence, decree light into my life. Amen.

DECREE NUMBER TWENTY-FOUR.

"On my bed I remember you, I think of you through the watches of the night"
Psalm 63:6.

Every day before I sleep, I remember you Lord in prayer and in petition. I call upon you for protection, mercy and favor. My thought is full of you. Before I sleep, my thoughts are loaded with meanings, but suddenly enemies appeared and distorted my sleep time table with arrow of emptiness. I am robbed of my dreams. Enemies lay me bare. I hardly remember my dreams. I am cornered before I knew it. Help me Lord, use your power and might to revive my dream life. Do not allow me to sleep like a dead dog waiting for unceremonial burial, that doesn't know what is going on around it.

Today, I am alive. In my sleep I shall be alive. My dreams shall magnetize into my brain. My brain box shall not be empty of dreams. Every spirit of blackout dwelling in my brain, and body shall die, in Jesus name I pray Amen.

PRAYER TO REMEMBER DREAMS

DECREE NUMBER TWENTY-FIVE.

"The Lions may grow weak and hungry, but those who seek the Lord lack no good thing"
Psalm 34:10.

Whose face shall I seek? Who can rescue me from the problems I face? It is my God. He is Jehovah EL-ASHIYB, the Lord my restorer. He shall restore what I lost in the past till this day. He shall restore my dream life without stress. My God shall fight this battle for me.

Really, Lions may grow weak and hungry; my hunger for dream restoration shall not hit the rock. My father shall refresh me and chase blackout from my system. O Lord, do not delay, do it today in Jesus name Amen.

DECREE NUMBER TWENTY-SIX.

"No King is saved by the size of his army, no warrior escapes by his great strength".
Psalm 33:16.

All power belong to God, He is the Almighty. Kings of this world may boast, yet they cannot match God. The size of their army cannot match God, their tricks have no meaning before the Lord. Oh Lord, my situation cry for emergency. Kings and warriors from the pit of hell ravaged my dream life. I am cornered before I knew it. They torment me in sleep and rob me of my virtues in the dream. Yet I don't know.

Empower me to regain my dream life. Let the promise spoken by Prophet Joel, in Joel 2:28 come to pass in my life. *"Your sons and daughters will prophesy, your old men will dream dreams, your young men will see vision"* I hardly dream, and when I dream, I forget all. My situation needs heavenly support. O Lord, defeat and destroy powers in charge of my dream problems. Amen.

PRAYER TO REMEMBER DREAMS

DECREE NUMBER TWENTY SEVEN

"Free me from the trap that is set for me, for you are my refuge".
Psalm 31:4.

Lord Jesus, I am caught in the trap of dream and forget. Enemies make mockery of me. They say, "We have got him" "He shall dream no more" "His memory is empty" "He is under spiritual blackout" But I know you can save me from the trap of the enemy.

Hasten Lord, and save me. Let me experience no blackout in my dream. Let me remember my dreams, give me spirit of understanding. Command fire to fall from heaven and consume witchcraft traps targeted against me in the name of Jesus. Amen.

DECREE NUMBER TWENTY-EIGHT

"Restore us, O God Almighty, make your face shine upon us, that we may be saved".
Psalm 80:7.

O Lord, restore me to perfection as you created me in the beginning, as you want me to be, and as you want me to fulfill my destiny. Enemies have concluded to pollute me against dreaming, or to remember my dreams. By this, my life is altered, my spirit being is affected.

O Lord, only one thing I demand from you, make your face shine upon me, save me from the hands of dark agents assigned against me. When you shine your eyes on me, my lost memory shall vanish and be blessed with new anointing that makes one remember his dreams. Therefore Lord, shine your eyes upon me to excel in life, in Jesus name I pray Amen.

DECREE NUMBER TWENTY-NINE.

"I sought the LORD, and he answered me, he delivered me from all my fears".
Psalm 34:4.

My God is never a destiny waster; rather He is a man of war. Whenever I seek for a thing, he answered me. Anytime I sought him my fears vanish. For this, I know I am delivered from the claws of the enemy. Here I am my Daddy in heaven; I come to you, for clear vision and dreams.

Rescue me from the hands of dark powers holding my vision to ransom. Clear traces of darkness in my memory bank. Refresh my thinking faculty. Give me power to remember my dreams vividly. O Heaven, grant my petition today, in Jesus name I pray, Amen.

DECREE NUMBER THIRTY.

"Ask of me, and I will make the nations your inheritance, the ends of the earth your possession"
Psalm 2:8.

O Lord, I ask for power to excel in life, and freedom from dream captivity. How can I inherit, if I can't communicate in dream with you Lord? Set me free today from chains of blackout harassing my sleep and dream life. I ask you this day Oh Lord empower me to dream and remember my dreams and possess my possessions.

Hence, I recover my spiritual senses from the claws of the enemy. My God shall command thunder and lightning from above to consume altar of darkness assigned to monitor my life.

PRAYER TO REMEMBER DREAMS

WARFARE AND BATTLE

DECREE NUMBER THIRTY ONE.

"O LORD, how many are my foes! How many rise up against me"!
Psalm 3:1.

My father and my God, enemies stoutly rise up against me to blacken and render my memory bank empty. They are foes and faceless agents of darkness. My dream life is under attack. Every time after sleep I record empty dreams. Your message to me is tampered with in the spirit.

It is the hand work of my foes that boast around saying, I can do but nothing. But with you, I am a winner. Empower me to counter their rise against me. Hence, I recover my dream senses today in the name of Jesus. Amen.

DECREE NUMBER THIRTY-TWO.

"And call upon me in the day of trouble, I will deliver you, and you will honor me"
Psalm 50:15

O Lord, come to my aid, great distress have taken over my sleep. Agents of darkness have taken me for granted; they polluted my dream at will. My memory is covered with deep darkness that makes me experience dream blackout.

Redeem my sleep O Lord from blankness. Perfect the beauty of my sleep, shine your light upon my destiny. Let my dream life have meaning. Empower me to remember my dreams. Give me wisdom as well, to interpret my dreams. Equip me with power to see vision. All honor belongs to you Lord, deliver me from the claws of enemies who are battle ready to deny me right to dreams. Pour anointing oil of excellence upon me; empower me to remember my dreams. So help me God, in Jesus name I pray Amen.

PRAYER TO REMEMBER DREAMS

DECREE NUMBER THIRTY-THREE

"My soul finds rest in God alone, my salvation comes from him. He alone is my rock and salvation; he is my fortress. I will never be shaken".
Psalm 62:1-2

With the Lord on my side I am a conqueror and shall recover my dream life. Enemies shall not trample upon me any longer. Dream devourer assigned against me shall die. They shall vomit what they devoured, from me in the name of Jesus.

I shall achieve this because the Lord is on my side. My God shall fight for me and I shall find rest in him. The Lord is my rock and salvation I shall never be shaken.

Lord Jesus be with me, rescue me from the spirit of dream and forget. Let your angels visit and keep watch over me, in Jesus name I pray Amen.

DECREE NUMBER THIRTY-FOUR.

"Send forth your light and your truth, let them guide me, let them bring me to your holy mountain, to the place where you dwell".
Psalm 43:3

O Lord send forth your light upon me. Let your revival power fall upon me. Let me arise above every power pulling me down in the spirit, visit my dream life. Pull me out of the valley to your holy mountain. Let me see clear vision. Let me have retentive memory of my dreams. To you O Lord, I surrender my case. Amen.

PRAYER TO REMEMBER DREAMS

DECREE NUMBER THIRTY-FIVE.

"Look on me and answer, O LORD my God. Give light to my eyes, or I will sleep in death: my enemy will say, "I have overcome him" and my foes will rejoice when I fall."
Psalm 13:3-4

The genesis of most downfalls, happen in the spirit. My eyes are equivalent to darkness when I sleep. I can't remember my visions and dreams. As a result, enemies rejoice because they know I can't communicate in the spirit. They laugh and look down on me in the spirit. They believe I am conquered.

O Lord, arise, give light to my eyes. Pull me out of the valley of death and valley of darkness. Let your anointing fall upon me. Let me regain my spiritual sight and memory in dreams and vision. Let your heavenly light shine upon my life. Let light occupy my memory bank. Let your light chase darkness out of me. Hence, I declare in the order of creation "Let there be Light" upon my destiny, and there is light that heals me of dream and forget syndrome. Amen.

DECREE NUMBER THIRTY SIX.
"The enemy pursues me, he crushes me to the ground, he makes me dwell in darkness like those long dead"
Psalm 143:3

My father and my God, I cry unto you, save me from the grip of the enemy. My dream life is at stake, a shadow of itself. It is at the mercy of dark powers. Mistakes, omissions and errors of mine caused me dream blackout. My sleep is like of a dead person. My sleep can best be described as empty, because I dream no more, I receive no spiritual message. When I dream, it is a matter of dream and forget. I am robbed of dreams.

Lord Jesus, appear in my sleep. Chase dream robbers away, paralyze their activities, destroy their plans. Place upon me banner of freedom, let dream touts around me scatter into desolation. So shall it be in Jesus name I pray. Amen.

DECREE NUMBER THIRTY-SEVEN.

"May the LORD cut off all flattering lips and every boastful tongue that says, "We will triumph with our tongues, we own our lips-who is our master?"
Psalm 12:3-4

My Lord, boastful tongues unleash curses and negative statements against my soul and sleep life. They boast I shall not remember my dreams any longer. They boast I shall dwell in the palace of dream world. I know you won't look elsewhere but save me. They boast, "We own our lip-who is our master?" I know, there is no other name above the name of Jesus. Therefore Lord, let them experience Holy Ghost slaps. Let them be put to shame. As to my memory, I recover you from captivity, in the name of Jesus. Amen.

DECREE NUMBER THIRTY-EIGHT.

"To you, O LORD, I lift up my soul, in you I trust, o my God. Do not let me be put to shame, not let enemies triumph over me"
Psalm 25:1-2.

My soul is for the LORD, powers of darkness shall not hold me. I pull myself from the hands of the wicked and gain my freedom by fire. Every spirit of the valley holding me captive shall die. I shall remember my dreams in full and interpretations them. Every enemy assigned to put me to shame as a result of dream and forget shall meet double failure. Every blackout in my life shall seize.

I am free from spiritual blackout. My God is with me, He shall decree goodness into my life from above. Hence, I receive decree of sound sleep and power to remember my dreams into my life. So help me God. Amen.

DECREE NUMBER THIRTY-NINE.

"They make their tongue as sharp as a serpent; the poison of a viper is on their lips"
Psalm 140:3.

O LORD, the tongue of the enemy rise sharply against me. My dream has been their target. They want to rob me of heavenly message. They gang up against my sleep. My joy to see vision and dream dreams is cut short. They captivate me with evil tongues. Their lips speak wickedness against me. They pollute my destiny without cause.

O LORD, may their plans against me scatter. May their glory refuse to shine. May their anger consume them. May their wicked skills meet double failure. May their wicked pregnancy against me be aborted. May darkness take over their activities. May their operations against me fail, in the name of Jesus.

The gear have changed in my favour. It is now dreams without struggle. My memory bank is sound and healthy. I shall remember my dreams now. I shall sing songs of praises to my Lord, for I shall dream and remember my dreams. Hence, I decree permanent joy and peace into my dream life. I decree dream fulfillment into my destiny. These, I claim in the name of Jesus. Amen.

DECREE NUMBER FOURTY.

"For with you is the fountain of life, in your light we see light"
Psalm 36:9.

Darkness is a palace of sorrow, setbacks, grief, terror and all forms of wickedness. It is one of the dwelling tools of Satan and his agents. My dream life is robbed through tools of darkness. Today, I hardly remember my dreams. But I know of someone who can redeem me from this. He shall bring light to my dwelling and destiny. I have hope in Him. His light overrides every other power. He is the Lord of lords and the King of kings. He is master Jesus.

O Lord redeem me from powers of darkness. Resurrect my dream life. Speak words of resurrection into my life. Let my dream life change for good. Every decree you pronounce from the heavenly to resurrect my dream life shall come to stay. Do it now O Lord. Amen.

PRAYER TO REMEMBER DREAMS

DECREE NUMBER FOURTY ONE.

"Set me free from my prison, that I may praise your name, then the righteous will gather about me because of your goodness to me"
Psalm 142:7.

Set me free O Lord, from the prison and captivity enemies placed me. Set me free from prison of dream blackout, prison of spiritual paralysis, prison of dream and forget, prison of poverty, prison of ungodliness, prison of anger, prison of backwardness and every form of prison, enemies placed me. Hence, I claim deliverance by fire as all prisons of darkness are dead. Amen.

DECREE NUMBER FOURTY TWO.

"As the dear pants for streams of water, so my soul pants for you, O God my soul thirsts for God, of the living God. When can I go and meet with God?"
Psalm 42:1-2.

My father and my God, I come before you as a man thirsty to remember his dreams. I am robbed of good things as I cannot remember my dreams. Even if evil is coming, I won't know. When blessings abound around me, I know not. For this reason, I come panting for the streams and rivers of dream that flows from your heavenly seat, as dear pants for streams of water when thirsty. I want you Lord, to destroy and kill every power responsible for the blackout ravaging my life.

With you Lord, I am a conqueror and a free person in the hands of the wicked. Your decree upon me to remember my dreams shall stand in the name of Jesus. Hence, my God shall empower me to remember my dreams, word for word and action for action, in the name of Jesus. Amen.

DECREE NUMBER FOURTY THREE.

"I cry to you, O Lord, I say, "You are my refuge, my portion in the land of the living" Listen to my cry, for I am in desperate need, rescue me from those who pursue me, for they are too strong for me"
Psalm 142:5-6.

Many are the calamities of the ungodly; many are the downfall of those far from God. I know, enemies encroached me when I was far inside dungeon of sins. But alas! My soul is awake! I walk out of dungeon of sin for the land of the living. As I determine to move, enemies refuse my take off.

With the power and support of the Almighty, I gained freedom for escape. Lord Jesus, I have gain freedom, but enemies are after me. They pursue me restlessly. They do not look back. O God, listen to my cry, for I am in desperate need, rescue me from those who pursue me, for they are too strong for me.
Hence, pronounce judgment against them, make a decree. Decree failure into their lives. Decree confusion into their gatherings. Let violence and destruction take them by surprise, as you decree success and understanding into my dream life. So help me God. Amen.

DECREE NUMBER FOURTY FOUR.

"Be merciful to me, O God, for men hotly pursue me, all day long they press their attack"
Psalm 56:1.

O Lord, save me from the hands of those that hotly pursue me and press attacks against my career, calling, business and know how. Lord Jesus, bear my burden, let owner of evil loads carry their loads. Let every evil load swallowing dreams in my life catch fire and roast to ashes. Let every enemy that joined forces to advance against me scatter. Let your sharp arrow pierce the heart of my stubborn pursuers. Instead of attacks in the dream, I shall record victory and outstanding progress in the name of Jesus.

Therefore Lord, decree success and wonders into my life. Your decree is final, pronounce it quickly Lord my life awaits you.

DECREE NUMBER FOURTY FIVE.

"Hide me from the conspiracy of the wicked, from that noisy crowd of evil doers".
Psalm 64:2.

With the power of the living God, I free my soul from the conspiracy of the wicked. I free my sleep from the attacks of powers from the pit of hell. I speak woe against every evil gang up molesting my sleep life. Every conspiracy assigned to render my dream memory useless shall meet double failure in the name of Jesus. Every curse pronounced against my memory shall backfire in the name of Jesus.

I hide under the protection of the Almighty. Noisy crowd of evil doers shall not locate me. No arrow of darkness shall locate me, either in the physical or in my sleep, in the name of Jesus. I pray Amen.

DECREE NUMBER FOURTY SIX.

"Send forth lightning and scatter the enemies, shout your arrows and rout them."
Psalm 144:6.

O Lord, I call unto you to send forth lightning from above and scatter enemies assigned against my dream. Let their gathering in the day and at night meet double failure. Let their plans scatter. Shoot your arrows O Lord and scatter them, for they gathered with evil intentions against me.

O Lord, do not look other way concerning my situation. As you scatter enemies against my dream life, let my memory bank resurrect by fire. Let wonders of dream and remember be my portion. Hence, I declare thus, "any time I dream, I shall remember it" in the name of Jesus. Amen.

DECREE NUMBER FOURTY SEVEN.
"I pursued my enemies and overtook them, I did not turn back till they were destroyed, I crushed them so that they could not rise, and they fell beneath my feet."
Psalm 18:37-38

Thou dark power that held to my virtues release them and die. Any power sitting upon my virtues I un-sit you by fire, therefore summersault and die in the name of Jesus. Hence, I pursue, overtake, overpower and destroy powers troubling my soul by the blood of the lamb. I possess my possession and rise above you. What you stole from me in the sleep I recover back by fire. I crush your head against Rock of Ages, never to rise again. I place you under permanent lock and key of the Almighty God. My God crush you never to rise again. You are therefore placed under my feet, forever and ever. Amen.

Hence I speak woe against every blackout introduced into my life. My memory bank is alive. I shall no longer forget my dreams again, in the name of Jesus. Amen.

DECREE NUMBER FOURTY EIGHT.

"May God arise, may his enemies be scattered, may his foes flee before him"
Psalm 68:1

Oh Lord my God, I am your son/daughter, harassed and humiliated in the dream by evil powers. I am your vessel on earth placed under dream captivity. I am the apple of your eyes seriously attacked by enemies in the sleep. Whoever attacks me, whichever power torments me, whatever means adopted to enslave me in the sleep is a slap on your face.

Therefore Lord, arise in your anger and let my enemies scatter. Let my foes flee before me. Let my memory bank function perfectly well and cause me to remember my dreams. Lord Jesus, decree dream breakthrough into my life. Let your Yes be Yes and your No remain No, concerning my life. To you Oh Lord, I rest my case. Amen.

DECREE FOURTY NINE.

"For as high as the heavens are above the earth so great is his love for those who fear him, as far as the east is from the west, so far has he removed our transgressions from us."
Psalm 103:11-12.

O Lord, envelope me with your love. Let me abide in righteousness so that I may be accepted before you. Arise to my situation fight this battle for me. Let your presence be felt in my life. As high as the heavens are above the earth, so shall enemies of my sleep be far from me. As far as the east is from the west, so far shall dream failure and arrow of dream and forget be far from me. Those that accuse me falsely to harm my dream shall meet double failure.

O Lord, satisfy my desires so that I may remember my dreams. Release me from captivity of dream failure, decree success into my life, in Jesus name I pray. Amen.

DECREE NUMBER FIFTY.

"As the mountains surround Jerusalem, so the LORD surrounds his people both now and forever more"
Psalm 125:2.

Thou Trinity, God the Father, God the Son, God the Holy Spirit, surround and protect me from wicked activities of dream criminals. They attack victims with arrow of blackout and deny me of my dreams. I know with divine supports, I will not be moved.

Holy Ghost, arrest every situation that cause forgetfulness in my life. Lord Jesus, use your blood like magnet, let my memory bank retain my dreams. I cry unto you Lord, save me from dream and forget situation. Visit me mightily; purge what caused it in my life. Do these speedily oh Lord, I rely on you. Amen.

PRAYER TO REMEMBER DREAMS

DECREE FIFTY ONE.

"I will lie down and sleep in peace, for you alone, O LORD, make me dwell in safety"
Psalm 4:8.

My safety resides with the Lord. I surrender my sleep to you O LORD. Let me experience victory and success in my dream. Let my memory bank reject spiritual blackout. Let joy fill me on daily basis. Let my comfort be, I dream and remember my dreams.

Any power assigned to torment my sleep shall die. Every instrument of darkness assigned against me shall catch fire and roast to ashes in the name of Jesus. My beddings shall be surrounded with fire of the Holy Ghost. Every assignment of the enemy to destroy my destiny shall meet double failure. I shall not record calamity in my sleep neither shall darkness take over my bed. Henceforth, I shall record peace and joy in my sleep in the name of Jesus. Amen.

DECREE NUMBER FIFTY TWO.

"But at your rebuke the waters fled, at the sound of your thunder they took to flight"
Psalm 104:7

Water cleanses, water washes, and water solves thirst as well. O Lord, I am thirsty to remember my dreams. I am thirsty for signs and wonders in my life. Use your heavenly water to cleanse my environ and destiny. Let contrary waters assigned against me dry up. Let wicked spirits that dwell in the water die. Paralyze their activities against my soul. Let heavenly thunder strike against them. Let them take to flight. Let their hunger to attack innocent souls work against them. Let my prayer be accepted before you this day. O Lord, save my sleep from the hands of the enemy so that your glory may shine upon my destiny.

Have fellowship with me O Lord; put an end to the attacks of the enemy. Anoint my head afresh. Let my dream memory be fresh. Give me wisdom to remember and understand my dreams. Let every arrow of dream and forget fired against me backfire by fire, in Jesus name I pray Amen.

Hence, I recover my dream life by fire for the anointing of the Lord is upon me. My God shall make me remember my dreams clearly, in the name of Jesus. Amen.

PRAYER TO REMEMBER DREAMS

DECREE NUMBER FIFTY-THREE.

"Though I walk in the midst of trouble, you preserve my life, you stretch out your hand against the anger of my foes, with your right hand you save me"
Psalm 138:7

Thou troublers of my Israel, my God shall trouble you. You encircle me with problems in dreams and deny me comfort in my sleep. You fire arrows against me and made me mere shadow on my bed. My long suffering is enough. I shall accept it no more.

For sometimes now, I dream, only to forget them all. My God preserves my life, only for dream criminals to torment me. My God stretched out his hands against the anger of my foes, only for them to re-group to torment me. O Lord, fulfill your purpose on me, do not look elsewhere as enemies torment me.

Hence, I decree liberty into my life. I decree failure against the works and attacks of the enemies. I decree joy in place of dream trauma. I decree boldness to fill my heart. I decree sound spirit to operate in my memory bank. I shall dream and remember, in the name of Jesus, I pray Amen.

DECREE NUMBER FIFTY-FOUR.

"You, O LORD, keep my lamp burning, my God turns my darkness into light. With your help I can advance against a troop, with my God I can scale a wall."
Psalm 18:28-29.

I fire arrow against every troop of darkness advancing against me. Every organized witchcraft against me shall scatter in the name of Jesus. Any power assigned to quench the lamp of God burning in me shall die. Light of God in me shall become visible. It shall give me testimonies, signs and wonders shall witness my prayer today.

The light of God shall chase darkness in me far away. Every darkness occupying my sleep shall vanish, because my God shall turn my darkness into light. By the power of the Almighty God, every stronghold keeping me in darkness shall die. I shall dream to remember my dreams in the name of Jesus, Amen.

PRAYER TO REMEMBER DREAMS

DECREE NUMBER FIFTY-FIVE.

"Let burning coals fall upon them, may they be thrown into the fire, into miry pits, never to rise" Psalm 140:10.

The plans of the enemy against me shall backfire at them. Their tricks shall be exposed. They shall enslave me no more in my sleep. Every arrow of blackout fired against me shall backfire. Their wicked thoughts shall bind them heavily; they shall be thrown into miry pits, never to rise again.

My God has fought the battle for me. I shall remember my dreams clearly. I am loaded with words of understanding in respect of my dreams. My dream life is re-generated, with back up of double fire. Revival has taken place in my life.

My dream life is unpolluted. My God has fought the battle for me. I shall not experience dream failure in my life anymore, so help me God. Amen.

DECREE NUMBER FIFTY-SIX.

"O Lord, how long will you look on? Rescue my life from their ravages, my precious life from these lions."
Psalm 35:17

Lord Jesus, King of glory, let your glory shine upon me. Lord Jesus, you are mighty in battle challenge and kill lions of darkness assigned against me. Holy Ghost, pronounce sudden death and defeat upon every wickedness holding my dream captive. Lord Jesus, walk into my life, heal the wounds in my life. Rebuild my memory bank afresh. Let every spirit of blackout in me die.

Lord Jesus, decree against evil lions chasing angels of blessings away from me. Let your power dwell in me. Empower me to recover from dream and forget saga. Henceforth, I shall abide under the shadow of the Almighty wings for ever and ever. Amen.

PRAYER TO REMEMBER DREAMS

DECREE NUMBER FIFTY-SEVEN.

"He raises the poor from the dust and lifts the needy from the ash heap".
Psalm 113:7.

Lord Jesus, give me peace beyond understanding. Draw me close to you and anoint my head. Command evil deposits in me to die. Render every evil pronunciation against me null and void. Deprogram every dark program assigned against me. Let your words be bread that nourishes me day and night. Let your blood be tonic that nourishes my body in the spirit. Let my head be treasure of your word and goodness that benefits human race.

Let your wonders reign in my life. Let your light take over every dark area in my life. Refine me O Lord, raise me to the level that will surprise many, lift me from the ash heap into palace of wonders.

Hence, my dream life shall be excellent while grace and wonders shall locate me, in Jesus name I pray Amen.

DECREE NUMBER FIFTY-EIGHT.

"Lift up your heads, O you gates, be lifted up, you ancient doors, that the King of glory may come in. Who is this King of glory? The LORD strong and mighty, the LORD mighty in battle".
Psalm 24:7-8.

Thou ancient gates and doors in charge of my destiny be lifted up and scatter. Let the storm of God dislocate you. Let your grip upon me meet double failure. The evils you planted in my dream life shall die and rise no more. Your foundations in my life shall be uprooted by fire. I command you to pack your loads off my destiny and die, in the name of Jesus.

Hence, I anoint my environment, my destiny and head with anointing oil of God. Everything around me shall be of God. My dream life shall change for better. I shall remember my dreams clearly because my God liveth. The King of glory shall establish goodness in my life. His glory shall shine upon my life. Amen.

DECREE NUMBER FIFTY-NINE.

"Let the slanderers not be established in the land, may disaster hunt down men of violence"
Psalm 140:11

Every power assigned to pull me down die. Every power monitoring my life for destruction is silenced. Thou power saying, I shall dream no more, run mad and die. Every attack against my dream life, scatter. Traps of darkness assigned to frustrate my life catch fire and roast to ashes. Arrow of God locate the bones of the enemy and scatter them by fire. Let disaster hunt down powers behind dream blackouts in my life.

My destiny is not for gambling; therefore I secure freedom by fire. I shall not wander aimlessly in dream kingdom. I shall uphold my dream and never forget my dreams anymore. Hence, I decree overflowing joy into my sleep and heavenly support for my prayers today. Amen.

DECREE NUMBER SIXTY.

"O God, the nations have invaded your inheritance, they have defiled your holy temple. They have reduced Jerusalem to rubble"
Psalm 79:1.

O Lord, enemies have invaded my destiny, they defile my body with evil foods. They never waste time but harass me with sex in the dream thereby polluting my sleep without cause. By this, they reduced me powerless and incompetent, I remember my dreams no more. I am but a shadow of myself now.

O Lord, perfect wonders in my life. Let powers and personalities assigned to wipe my dream meet double failure. Hence, announce your glory, and favor upon my life, now and forever more, Amen.

PRAYER TO REMEMBER DREAMS

DECREE NUMBER SIXTY-ONE.

"May all who hate Zion be turned back in shame, may they be like grass on the roof, which withers before it can grow"
Psalm 129:5-6.

Enemies hate people with dream accuracy and this is what I thirst for, hence enemies hate me. Therefore Lord, strike them on the jaw, baptize them with blindness, and turn them back in shame. May their days be numbered. May they be like grass that grow on the roof which withers before it can grow.

May their household go into desolation; may their labor be in vain? May their strength wither, may they be confused in the dream. May their finances meet doom and sudden liquidation.

As from today, they shall record failure upon failure concerning my issues. In the dream, I shall defeat them, in the physical; they shall experience failure as well. Every arrow fired against me shall backfire and consume them, in Jesus name I pray, Amen.

DECREE NUMBER SIXTY-TWO.

"They swamped around me like bees, but they died out as quickly as burning thorns, in the name of the LORD I cut them off."
Psalm 118:12.

O Lord, let every conspiracy against me scatter. Let enemies that swamped around me like bees die one by one. Turn me to live wire and let any dark power that touches me in my sleep catch fire and roast to ashes. If blood suckers come close at me let your divine fire electrocute them. Don't allow my enemies know peace until they vacate my life. Grant me success in my sleep.

As I cry to you O Lord in anguish, set me free. Let me look with triumph over my enemies with joy. Disgrace evil agents who are battle ready to steal my dream message. Free me from chains of darkness. Let me arise above dream failure. In the name of Jesus.

PRAYER TO REMEMBER DREAMS

DECREE NUMBER SIXTY-THREE

"I will not die but live, and will proclaim what the LORD has done."
Psalm 118:17

My Lord made his light shine upon me. Every arrow fired against me shall backfire. Every altar of darkness where my name is mentioned shall catch fire and burn to ashes. Every attack against me in the dream shall meet double failure. Every gathering of the enemy assigned to foment evil against me shall scatter. Enemies that pursued me in my sleep shall fall by the sword.

My God shall wipe my tears. He shall give me peace beyond understanding. He shall draw me close to Himself and anoint my head against every form of dream pollution. My days of joy have come, I shall overcome every form of dream attack. I have no cause to fear in the dream because the protection and love of God is upon me. Henceforth, I shall witness joy, favor and mercy of God in my sleep for ever and ever. Amen.

DECREE NUMBER SIXTY-FOUR

"Even in the darkness light downs for the upright, for the gracious and compassionate and righteous man."
Psalm 112:4.

O Lord, revive me and clear darkness in my life. Let your light shine and disgrace every darkness holding me captive. Let powers of darkness disappear in my life. Speak woe against every power and personality using dark powers as cover for me in the dream. Let your anointing on me frighten wicked powers to submission. Make me mighty before my enemies. Let your power cleanse my memory bank of every form of pollution.

As from today, my God shall make me remember my dreams, never to forget it after sleep. Amen.

PRAYER TO REMEMBER DREAMS

DECREE NUMBER SIXTY-FIVE.

You are my refuge and my shield, I have put my hope in your word. Away from me, you evildoers, that I may keep the commands of my God! Psalm 119:114-115.

My father and my God, I come to you for safety from the hands of night raiders. They raid my sleep at will and cause me nightmare. My sleep is not sweet but full of sorrow. My dreams are polluted, I hardly remember them. They gang up against my sleep. My communication with heaven is either blocked or polluted. I hardly hear from heaven. All these, are the handwork of evildoers, who are bent in robbing me of my dreams.

Away from me, you evildoers so that I may have good dreams in my sleep.
Away from me, you evildoers that I may have total freedom from the pit of hell.
Away from me, you evil doers that I may reap joy after sleep.
Away from me, you evildoers, for your time is up.
Away from me, you evildoers, for my God has passed judgment against you.
Hence, I decree heavenly support for my prayers, in the name of Jesus. Amen.

DECREE NUMBER SIXTY-SIX.

"They who seek my life will be destroyed; they will go down to the depth of the earth."
Psalm 63:9.

Holy Ghost arise with zeal and power, fight and rescue me from the hands of the wicked. Let your spirit dwell in me to withstand and kill night raiders assigned against me. Let their instrument of destruction work against them by fire. Guide me from the ruthless attitude of dream killers in the sleep. Let those who seek my life be destroyed.

Let them go down to the depths of the earth. Let their gang up against me scatter. Destroy them before they destroy me, in Jesus name I pray. Amen.

DECREE NUMBER SIXTY-SEVEN.

"They make their tongue as sharp as a serpent, the poison of a viper is on their lips"
Psalm 140:3.

O LORD, the tongue of the enemy rise sharply against me. My dream has been their target. They want to rob me of heavenly message. They gang up against my sleep. My joy to see vision and dream dreams is cut short. They captivate me with evil tongues. Their lips speak wickedness against me. They pollute my destiny without cause.

O LORD, may their plans against me scatter. May their glory refuse to shine. May their anger consume them. May their evil skills meet double failure. May their wicked pregnancy against me be aborted. May darkness take over their activities. May their operations against me fail, in the name of Jesus.

The gear has changed in my favour. It is now dreams without struggle. My memory bank is sound and healthy. I shall remember my dreams now. I shall sing songs of praises to my Lord, for I shall dream and remember my dreams. Hence, I decree permanent joy and peace into my dream life. I decree dream fulfillment into my destiny. These, I claim in the name of Jesus. Amen.

DECREE NUMBER SIXTY-EIGHT.

"The day is yours, and yours also the nights, you established the sun and moon"
Psalm 74:16

O Lord, all days are yours but I am troubled day by day by agents of darkness who are bent at destroying me. Every second, every minute, every hour, every day are yours. Yet on daily basis, I am molested by dream criminals. They raid my sleep at will and harass me time without number. They encouraged themselves more and more as they carry out evil against my sleep. My destiny is far troubled. They hotly pursue me in the dream and refuse to let me enjoy my sleep.

O Lord arise, let the sun speak against them; let the moon work against their activities. Rebuke these nasty powers, chain them down without delay.

PRAYER TO REMEMBER DREAMS

DECREE NUMBER SIXTY-NINE.

"Let the wicked fall into their own nets, while I pass by in safety"
Psalm 141:10.

Enemies created nets of different shapes and sizes to entangle me. They perfected their acts for evil. They came from pit of hell to torment evil against me. They mess me up in dreams and harass me to submission. I wake to remember my dreams, but experience failure. I cannot remember my dreams.

My Lord and My God, afflict powers behind my predicaments with madness. Let the wicked fall into their own nets. Turn their environment into thick darkness they can't operate. Make their paths slippery. Let them fall into pits they cannot rise from. Let them be put into double shame.

Decree from your holy seat against their existence O Lord. Let pillars they held fall upon them. Let destruction take them by surprise. Let affliction consume them. Hence, I decree success in my dream and peace in my sleep, so help me God. Amen.

DECREE NUMBER SEVENTY.

"Let death take my enemies by surprise, let them go down alive to the grave, for evil finds lodging among them".
Psalm 55:15

Those who attack me in the sleep don't want me to realize my goals in life. They are enemies of progress that wants me to crawl rather than walk. They want me to bite fingers in vain. Their plans is to drag me on the floor in shame, But my God refused their plans to work out.

O Lord, scatter the bones of the wicked, spray them with perfume of rejection. Break every covenant that exist between me and them. Pronounce decree of restoration into my life. Baptize me with dream miracles and understanding. Restore my hope O Lord; let your fortunes flourish in my life. Unto you I cry O Lord. Amen.

PRAYER TO REMEMBER DREAMS

DECREE NUMBER SEVENTY-ONE

"Why do you boast of evil, you mighty man? Why do you boast all day long, you who are a disgrace in the eyes of God?"
Psalm 52:1.

The boast of the ungodly is empty before the Lord, and of no effect before the righteous. The boast of the wicked shall bring disgrace unto them. Their boasts shall bring them low. Their boasts shall hold no water in my life. The boast of, "I have conquered his/her dream life" shall not come to pass in my life.

Hence, I recover my dream life by fire. I shall remember my dreams now and forever more.

DECREE NUMBER SEVENTY-TWO.

"The LORD watches over you – the LORD is your shade at your right hand, the sun will not harm you by day, nor the moon by night"
Psalm 121:5-6.

Lord Jesus, come to my aid, help me out of dream and forget problems. The psalmist says you shall watch over me, but enemies kept bombarding me with fragmented and dream blackouts. This has disrupted my spiritual growth. No spiritual message sticks to my brain, I remember nothing after sleep. My dreams life is shaking.

Lord Jesus, be my shade and protector against dream vandals that torment me at will. Be a shade unto me 24 hours every day. Do not allow sun harm me by day, nor the moon by night. To you **O LORD** I cry for help. Revive my dream life. Let me remember my dreams now and forever more, Amen.

DECREE NUMBER SEVENTY-THREE.

"For the Lord will rebuild Zion and appear in his glory. He will respond to the prayer of the destitute, he will not despise their plea."
Psalm 102:16-17.

O Lord, restore the glory of the old, visit my foundation for signs and wonders. Let your glory shine upon my destiny. Let my prayer be accepted before you this day. Have fellowship with me O Lord, put an end to attacks of the enemy. Anoint my head afresh. Let my dream memory be fresh.

O Lord despise my dreams no more. Give me wisdom and understanding to remember my dreams. Let every arrow of dream and forget fired against me backfire by fire in Jesus name, I pray. Amen.

DECREE NUMBER SEVENTY-FOUR.

"Arise, O LORD! Deliver me, O my God! Strike all my enemies on the jaw; break the teeth of the wicked"
Psalm 3:7

O Lord, it is time you come to my aid. Do not allow wicked powers assigned to empty my dream go un-punished. I am denied my divine right, the right to communicate through dream with your heavenly seat. O Lord, strike all enemies that torment my sleep on the jaw, break the teeth they used to molest me. Deliver my memory from evil supervision and control.

Hence, I command freshness into my sleep. I command freshness into my dream. I shall forget my dreams no more in the name of Jesus I pray. Amen.

PRAYER TO REMEMBER DREAMS

DECREE NUMBER SEVENTY FIVE.

"Arise, O LORD, in your anger, rise up against the rage of my enemies. Awake, my God, decree justice"
Psalm 7:6

O Lord, let your anger rise against powers injecting failure into my destiny. Load me with power to counter every rage of the enemy. O Lord, decree justice of liberty, decree justice of restoration, decree justice of favor and sleep well upon my life.

Let my groans and complaints of dream and forget come to an end today. Let your fire of revival visit memory bank of my life. In your anger purge me of evil deposit and make me dwell in peace. Let this be O LORD, for your justice is final. Amen.

DECREE NUMBER SEVENTY-SIX

It is written, *"Let the heads of those who surround me be covered with the trouble their lips have caused"*
Psalm 140:9.

Angels of the Living God arise and take position around me. In my sleep, do not sleep off, do not roam about, do not be weak vessels before powers troubling my sleep. Enemies have spoken evil words against my sleep. They fired arrow at me at will.

Therefore, let the heads of those who surround me be covered with the trouble their lips have caused. Wherever they gathered scatter them. Whatever evil they speak against me, let it backfire at them. Let their heads experience double tragedy.

My father and my God, decree affliction and terror upon them. Let shame catch up with them. Let them be helpless in my matters. Let blackout planted in me expire today. I am free from memory loss, I shall remember my dreams all over, in Jesus name I pray Amen.

PRAYER TO REMEMBER DREAMS

DECREE NUMBER SEVENTY-SEVEN.

O Sovereign LORD my strong deliverer, who shields my head in the day of battle-do not grant the wicked their desires, O LORD, do not let their plans succeed, or they will become proud"
Psalm 140:7-8.

My father and my God, arise to my situation, save me from the hands of the wicked that torments me day and night. Deliver me from the grip of sleep polluter. Deliver me from dream rascals who never want me to excel in life. Deliver me from demonic sleep do not allow me sleep a sleep of death. Rulers of darkness want me to sleep like a dead dog who knows nothing that happens around it.

Therefore Lord, arise! I say arise, revive my dream life. Let your arrow locate the camp of the enemy and scatter them. Let your anger rise against them speedily. Let their plans against me scatter. I spread out my hands to you O Lord, my soul thirsts for dreams from above.

Hence, I decree as follows: - May my heavenly father support me to remember my dreams. May angels of God guide and support me from the attacks of dream criminals. May my habitation be guided with fire of the Holy Ghost, so shall it be in Jesus name, Amen.

CONFESSIONS OF POSSESSION

DECREE NUMBER SEVENTY EIGHT.

"For great is your love toward me, you have delivered me from the depths of the grave"
Psalm 86:13

Who is mighty than my Lord? Who can withstand Him? He set the Israelites free from bondage. They crossed the Red Sea un hurt. They crushed their enemies in the wilderness. They occupied the Promised Land and laid record no nation ever had.

The same God is the One I call upon today. He shall save me from the claws of my enemies. I shall no longer be a victim in their hands. My dream life shall come back by fire. My memory bank shall experience spiritual revival. I shall be a winner and not a loser. No power shall trample upon me any longer. My God is solidly behind me. I shall not dream and forget anymore. Hence forth, I shall remember my dreams clean and clear in the name of Jesus. Amen.

"When the LORD brought back the captives to Zion, we were like men who dreamed. Our mouths were filled with laughter, our tongues with songs of joy"
Psalm 126:1-2.

PRAYER TO REMEMBER DREAMS

Praise the Lord Almighty, the omnipresent God, who is always present and concerned with situations. The I AM that I AM, who lives forever, the Omniscience God, who knows everything. The Alpha and the Omega, who knows the beginning and the ending of everything that concerns me. He is Jehovah Go'eleck- The Lord is redeemer, He is Jehovah Ori- The Lord is my light. He shown bright light into my situation and set me free from dream blackout. My memory bank is resurrected from dark powers and commands of dark kingdom. I am free and free indeed.

At last, my mouth is filled with laughter, for I shall remember my dreams now. My God made me to burst into laughter over my enemies as I remember my dreams. My days of agony are gone; my tongue is full of songs of joy. I shall sing, sing and sing unto the Lord, because I regain my dream life back. Praise the Lord Almighty who did it in my life. Amen.

"Shout for joy to the Lord, all the earth, burst into jubilant song with music."
Psalm 98:4

- I will shout with joy unto my Lord, who rescued me from problems, who rescued me from dream blackout. Blood of Jesus washed my dream bank clean from every form of spiritual blackout. My head is anointed afresh. This day I am not a victim of night raiders and powers that rob people of their rights in sleep. I am free, and free indeed praise the Lord. Halleluiah. Amen.

PRAYER TO REMEMBER DREAMS

DECREE NUMBER SEVENTY NINE.

"But you are a shield around me, O LORD; you bestow glory on me and lift up my head"
Psalm 3:3.

O Lord my God, be a shield around me 24 hours of the day. Guide and guard my sleep. Bestow your glory upon me and lift up my head. Let your angels be my guard while I sleep. Let your angels strike down any dark agent assigned to corrupt, steal or cause me blockage from receiving my heavenly message.

I say once again Lord, let your glory shine on me. Lift up my head against the match of evil ones. My head, receive deliverance and power to record heavenly messages. I release you from the captivity of memory loss in the name of Jesus. Amen.

DECREE NUMBER EIGHTY

"They band together against the righteous and condemn the innocent to death."
Psalm 94:21.

Night raiders are heartless, looking for whom to devour in sleep. They devour dreams of many and cause blackout in their memories. They ensure defeat of victims in the spirit and render them helpless in the physical. They form bands against the righteous looking for how to pollute them. Many foundations are ruined this way.

But I call upon the Lord to fight my battle and make me glorious. Hence, with the Lord, on my side, I shall have cause to remember my dreams. Amen.

PRAYER TO REMEMBER DREAMS

DECREE NUMBER EIGHTY-ONE.

"For in the day of trouble he will keep me safe in his dwelling, he will hide me in the shelter of his tabernacle and set me high upon a rock."
Psalm 27:5.

Upon the rock of the Lord I stand as a gallant soldier of the Lord. My troubles are in trouble; my problems are in for it. Therefore spirit of blackout in me shall die. Spirit of dream and forget in me shall die. They have nowhere to hide in my life any longer, as Holy Ghost Fire shall burn them to ashes.

The Lord is my shelter; his tabernacle is my dwelling place. My dream memory is alive. I shall remember every bit of my dreams clearly in the name of Jesus. Lord Jesus, you are the Rock of Ages, in whom I hide. Amen.

Sing this song
THE LORD THAT NEVER FAIL
LET ME HIDE IN YOU
LET ME HIDE IN YOU
IN YOU THERE IS POWER.

Henceforth, I am free of dream and forget. My Lord has anointed my head afresh. My memory bank shall not experience pollution any longer. I am free, in Jesus name. Amen.

DECREE NUMBER EIGHTY-TWO

"We have escaped like a bird out of the fowler's snare, the snare has been broken, and we have escaped"
Psalm 124:7.

O Lord, I thank you for wanders that shall take place in my life, after agony of dream and forget for several years. With faith and believe I am free from dream captivity. I am like a bird out of the fowler's snare. I gained freedom from long-term captivity. Dream erasers assigned against me missed it all. They are failures. Their tricks and methods to erase my dreams hit the rock!

The snare of the enemy against my dream is broken. Sex in the dream has vacated my life. Dark veils against me caught fire and roast to ashes. Eating in the dream is gone and gone forever.

My memory bank is revived. Every dream attack is placed under control by the Almighty, in the name of Jesus. Amen.

PRAYER TO REMEMBER DREAMS

DECREE NUMBER EIGHTY-THREE.

"I will praise you, O LORD, with all my heart, I will tell of all your wonders. I will be glad and rejoice in you, I will sing praise to your name. O MOST HIGH".
Psalm 9:1-2.

The wonders of the Lord shall manifest in my life. His wonders has added value to my dream life. My memory bank is revived; wicked deposits in me are dead. Wonders in the order of Daniels understanding is deposited in me. Therefore, I shall remember and be able to interpret my dreams. Songs of praise shall ever be in my mouth. So help me God. Amen.

DECREE NUMBER EIGHTY-FOUR.

"Praise to the LORD my ROCK, who trains my hands for war, my fingers for battle"
Psalm 144:1.

My Lord is my Rock; the one I relied to revive my dream life. He shall pull me out of the pit and valley of darkness. He shall see me through and end dream and forget troubling my soul. He shall issue decree against blackout in my life.

Special announcement! My God has trained my hands for war, therefore, any aggression against me shall scatter by fire. He strengthens my hands with heavenly anointing to excel as a champion. My hands shall pull down strongholds of the enemy.

My fingers are not left out! He trains my fingers for battles. They go into actions and win battles. I shall realize my goal. I shall dream and remember my dreams. Hence, I decree against dream blackout in Jesus name I pray, Amen.

PRAYER TO REMEMBER DREAMS

DECREE NUMBER EIGHTY FIVE

"My God, my God, why have you forsaken me? Why are you so far from saving me, so far from the words of my groaning?"
Psalm 22:1

Lord Jesus, my groan and spiritual blackout is becoming unbearable, come to my aid and help me out. My sleep has no meaning to me; communication link through dream is polluted. Spiritual vandals kept me captive. I shout unto you this day to save me from the spirit of dream and forget. Hence, I recover my spiritual senses; valor and wisdom to remember and interpret my dream. I shall not record failure again in my sleep.

Every burden supervising and or tormenting my sleep life shall die in the name of Jesus. My memory bank is released from the captive of the enemy. Amen. So help me Lord.

DECREE NUMBER EIGHTY-SIX.

"To you I call, O LORD my ROCK, do not turn deaf ear to me. For if you remain silent, I will be like those who have gone down to the pit."
Psalm 28:1.

My Lord is my creator, I am his child. Every good thing I ask my God, He gives me. My Lord gives listening ear to me, all I need to do is give him listening ears. Hence Lord, I cry unto you for mercy, miracle signs and wonders. Let your power reign in my dream life. Let your angels guide me in my sleep from night raiders. Let every confrontation against my sleep die.

Install divine computer in my brain. Whatever you reveal to me in my sleep shall be known to me until I am satisfied. My God shall do according to my plea. He will not turn deaf ear to me in the name of Jesus. Amen.

PRAYER TO REMEMBER DREAMS

DECREE NUMBER EIGHTY SEVEN.

"A righteous man may have many troubles, but the LORD delivers him from them all."
Psalm 34:19

My boast is not of righteousness for my Lord shall sanctify me. I am a new creature, blended into righteousness by my father in heaven. I shall not walk into sin, dance with sin or go into sin anymore. My God shall empower me for this, for it is not by power or might I do it. With my garment of righteousness in me, I possess my dream life by fire. Every plantation of darkness in me that makes me forget my dreams shall die.

Every spirit collecting my dreams or waving it aside shall die. My memory bank shall not dry or be blank. O Lord let your power of resurrection fall upon my dream life, in Jesus name I pray, Amen.

DECREE NUMBER EIGHTY-EIGHT.

"When the LORD brought back the captives to Zion, we were like men who dreamed. Our mouths were filled with laughter, our tongues with songs of joy"
Psalm 126:1-2.

Praise the Lord Almighty, the omnipresent God, who is always present and concerned with situations. The I AM that I AM, who lives forever, the Omniscience God, who knows everything. The Alpha and the Omega, who knows the beginning and the ending of everything that concerns me. He is Jehovah Go'eleck- The Lord is redeemer, He is Jehovah Ori- The Lord is my light. He shown bright light into my situation and set me free from dream blackout. My memory bank is resurrected from dark powers and commands of dark kingdom. I am free and free indeed.

At last, my mouth is filled with laughter, for I shall remember my dreams now. My God made me to burst into laughter over my enemies as I remember my dreams. My days of agony are gone; my tongue is full of songs of joy. I shall sing, sing and sing unto the Lord, because I regain my dream life back. Praise the Lord Almighty who did it in my life. Amen.

DECREE NUMBER EIGHTY-NINE

"Shout for joy to the Lord, all the earth, burst into jubilant song with music."
Psalm 98:4

I will shout with joy unto my Lord, who rescued me from problems, who rescued me from dream blackout. Blood of Jesus washed my dream bank clean from every form of spiritual blackout. My head is anointed afresh. This day I am not a victim of night raiders and powers that rob people of their rights in sleep. I am free, and free indeed praise the Lord. Halleluiah. Amen.

DECREE NUMBER NINETY.

"Your word is a lamp to my feet and a light to my path."
Psalm 119:105.

O Lord, let your lamp be a light upon me, upon my sleep, upon my bed and upon my destiny. With your lamp, I shall fear no evil, for no arrow shall locate me. Your light disgraced darkness in my life. It places permanent padlock in the mouth of the enemy. They become dumb, un-operative and useless in their nocturnal activities. Your light paralyzed their hands and legs.

As your love and faithfulness abides in my sleep Lord, let my enemies turn back from attacking me in the name of Jesus. Amen.

PRAYER TO REMEMBER DREAMS

DECREE NUMBER NINETY-ONE.

"I will praise the LORD, who counsels me; even at night my heart instructs me. I have set the LORD always before me. Because he is at my right hand, I will not be shaken."
Psalm 16:7-8

I claim victory over spiritual blackout of the brain. Even at night and in sleep my heart and senses instructs me. I shall forget my dreams no more because my LORD is at my right hand, giving commands against powers that may molest me in my sleep. My agony is over. I shall experience dreams with accuracy. I will not be shaken; fear of the night is dead in my life.

I have a living memory bank of dreams now! I shall recount my dreams one be one without fear any longer. I am blessed in Jesus name. Amen.

DECREE NUMBER NINETY-TWO.

"But I am like an olive tree flourishing in the house of God, I trust in God's unfailing love for ever and ever."
Psalm 52:8.

The anointing of the Lord is upon me. It shall be permanent. I shall excel in my sleep, career and calling in the name of Jesus. What I lost through dream I shall recover. I shall flourish in life without negation. The love of God upon me shall not die. My God shall open my eyes for visions. He shall prefect my dream from pollution. Those who trouble me shall be troubled in the name of Jesus, Amen.

PRAYER TO REMEMBER DREAMS

DECREE NUMBER NINETY-THREE.

"May the LORD, the Maker of heaven and earth, bless you from Zion" Psalm 134:3.

O Lord, the maker of heaven and earth, decree good things into my life, command blessings to flow in my favor. Hence, I decree as follows into my life.

May my sleep be blessed in the name of Jesus.
May my dreams be blessed in the name of Jesus.
May my prayer be blessed in the name of Jesus.
May the praises and thanksgiving that proceed from my mouth be blessed in the name of Jesus.
May the faith I have in the Lord in this prayer be blessed in the name of Jesus.
May the strength in me be blessed in the name of Jesus.
May my habitation be blessed in the name of Jesus.
May my coming and going out be blessed in the name of Jesus.
May my household be blessed in the name of Jesus.
May my finances be blessed in the name of Jesus.
May my career be blessed in the name of Jesus.
May the Lord Almighty bless me mightily.
May I be lifted beyond human imaginations.
May my dreams not deceive me any day.

May God give me deep understanding to interpret my dreams error free. May the Lord uphold me, forever and ever, amen.

DECREE NUMBER NINETY FOUR.

"He put a new song in my mouth, a hymn of praise to our God. Many will see and fear and put their trust in the LORD"
Psalm 40:3.

New song shall burst forth from my mouth this day. My fear concerning dream and forget is over. I shall no longer record zero or partial dreams again. I am set free from the bondage of dream and forget. My destiny shall witness sudden turn around for good. People that thought I am spiritually dead shall have cause to shut up. I have won the battle against dream failure. I am a new creature in the Lord, so shall it be in Jesus name. Amen.

DECREE NUMBER NINETY-FIVE.

"Let Israel rejoice in their Maker, let the people of Zion be glad in their King"
Psalm 149:2.

I (*mention your name*) shall rejoice in the Lord my Maker. He knew what I passed through and came to my aid. He saw I was robbed in the dream; he put a stop to it. I was denied access to dream kingdom, he stopped it. I can dream and remember my dreams now. How many shall I count? Sex in the dream vanished in my life. Veils of darkness vanished from the corridor of my life. Wicked bands loosed by fire and roast to ashes. I experience dream blackout no more. I have cause to rejoice in the LORD, for he did wonders in my life.

My family has cause to rejoice and be glad, for I shall complain no more. My friends have cause to rejoice with me, for I shall question them no more. I say, everybody rejoice with me, I am now a new creature, my memory bank has resurrected, I shall dream and remember all. Praise the Lord. Hallelujah.

DECREE NUMBER NINETY-SIX.

"You turned my wailing into rejoicing, you removed my sackcloth and clothed me with joy." Psalm 30:11.

My heart shall sing and rejoice unto to the Lord, for what he did in my life today. He ended my grief and sorrow of dream and forget. He empowers me to remember my dreams. The era of blackout is over. I cross over to dream land and say bye to the land of dream blackout. So shall it be in Jesus name. Amen.

DECREE NUMBER NINETY SEVEN

"Weeping may remain for a night, but rejoicing comes in the morning"
Psalm 30:5b.

My weep over dream failure shall come to end today. My lamentation over dream and forget is over. I overcome trouble of blackout like flash of lightning. Blackout is gone in my life; my Lord fought the battle for me. My faith in the Lord is as strong as ever. When trouble comes, with faith in the Lord, I overcome it. This is the situation now. I have won the battle over dream and forget. So shall it be forever and ever. Amen.

PRAYER TO REMEMBER DREAMS

DECREE NUMBER NINETY EIGHT.

"Praise the LORD. Sing to the LORD a new song, his praise in the assembly of the saints" Psalm 149:1

I praise you O Lord my God.
You are wonderful in listening to people's request.
Anyone who comes to you leave with joy.
Joy, peace, riches, love are yours.
My joy is full as you chase spirit of blackout from my life.
My heart is comforted with heavenly message.
I shall sing unto you time without number.
Songs of victory shall find place in my mouth.
Songs of spiritual breakthrough are mine.
My God decree in heaven concerning me.
That I am free from dream blackout
Dream erasers fled my life.
Hosanna is the highest.
Messiah is God.
Hallelujah.

DECREE NUMBER NINETY-NINE.

1. Praise the Lord
Praise the LORD from the heavens,
Praise Him in the heights above
2. Praise him, all his angels.
Praise him, all his heavenly hosts.
3. Praise him, sun and moon,
Praise him, all you shining stars.
Psalm 148:1-3.

I will praise my LORD, for the wonders he did in my life. I will praise Him, in respect of my dream life. I will praise Him, as I shall experience "operation dream and remember" and "operation clear dream, clear remembrance", in the name of Jesus.

Era of blackout vacates my life. Dream rascals vacate my life. Dream erasers saw me and fled. Dream criminals fold their hands to their chest in shame. They watch me in awe at distance. What a marvelous glory God gave me before my enemies.

The heavens are happy concerning my case. The angels dance in heaven for my sake. Heavenly hosts smiles in my support. The sun and the moon, praise my God as well. The stars are not left out, as they praise God. To you be the glory, my LORD and my God. Amen.

FINAL THANKSGIVING

At last, my prayers are answered. I shall not be disgraced. My God is mighty behind me. I have recovered from dream and forget syndrome. My joy is full. Laughter finally locates my mouth. My vision shall be clear as in the order of the prophets of the old. God has visited my foundation for good. I am now a champion, and shall never be a failure in the territory of dreams. So help me God. Amen.

O Lord, I thank you for the wonderful hands you laid upon me. I thank you for giving me listening ears. I thank you for mercy and favor I received from you this day. I thank you because I recover from dream and forget syndrome. O Lord, I thank you once again, in Jesus name I pray. Amen.

YOU HAVE BATTLES TO WIN

TRY THESE BOOKS

1. COMMAND THE DAY

Each day of the week is loaded with meanings and divine assurance. God did not create each day of the week for the fun of it. Blessings, success, gifts, resources, hopes, portfolios, duties, rights, prophecy, warnings and challenges, are loaded in each day. Do you know the language, command or decree you can use to claim what belongs to you in each day of the week? Do you know in Christendom, Monday can be equated to one of the days of creation in Genesis chapter one? Do you know creation lasted for six days and God rested on the seventh day? What day of the week can Christian equate as the first day of the week, if we follow Christian calendar? What day can we call day seven? This book shall give insight to these questions. It shall explain how you can command each day of the week according to creation in the book of Genesis chapter one. Above all, you shall exercise your right and claim what is hidden in each day. Check for this in **COMMAND THE DAY**

2 FIRE FOR FIRE PRAYER BOOKS PARTS 1&2

These prayer books are fast at answering spiritual problems. They are bulldozer prayer books, full of prayers all through. They are highly recommended for night vigil. Testimonies are pouring in daily from users of these books across the world!

3. PRAYER FOR FRUIT OF THE WOMB
This prayer book is children magnet By faith and believe in God Almighty, as soon as you use this book open doors to child bearing shall be yours. Amen

4. PRAYER FOR PREGNANT WOMEN.
This a spiritual prayer book loaded with prayers of solution for pregnant women. As soon as you take in, the prayers you shall pray from day one of conception to delivery day are written in this book.

5. WARFARE IN OFFICE
It is high time you pray prayers of power must change hands in office. Use this book and liberate yourself from every form of office yoke.

6. MY MARRIAGE SHALL NOT BREAK
Marriage is corner piece of life, happiness and joy. You need to hold it tight and guide it from wicked intruders and destroyer of homes.

7. VICTORY OVER SATANIC HOUSE 1 & 2
Are you a tenant, Land lord bombarded left and right, front and back by wicked people around you?

TELLA OLAYERI

With this book you shall be liberated from the hooks of the enemy.

PRAYER TO REMEMBER DREAMS

For Further Enquiries Contact
**THE AUTHOR
EVANGELIST TELLA OLAYERI**
P.O. Box 1872 Shomolu Lagos.
Tel: 08023583168

FROM AUTHOR'S DESK

Authors write for others to digest, gain and broaden intellects. Your comment is therefore needed to arouse others into Christ's bosom.

I therefore implore you to comment on this on this book.

God bless.

Thanks.

Printed in Great Britain
by Amazon